"Once again, Bryan _____, Prince gives us one more great story of an unsung hero. He is the consummate historian, continually uncovering exciting adventures of international connections of people of African descent.

"His thirty-year unquenchable thirst for answers to his ancestors is amazing. The number of sources Prince used, the number of experts he consulted, the geography he covered sleuthing out the story, and the years spent researching Isaac Brown is astounding.

"Whereas historians and genealogists are always looking for sources, following Prince's journey through archives in Canada and the U.S. reveal the voluminous sources that are available after continuously hitting brick walls and dead ends. With all the original sources that have not been digitized, Bryan's journey continually reminds me of the fallacy of the 'end of the paper trail.'"

— **Tony Burroughs**, Fellow of the Utah Genealogical Society (FUGA) and author of the bestselling *Black Roots: A Beginner's Guide to Tracing the African-American Family Tree*

"Once again, Bryan Prince, intrepid historian and masterful storyteller, brings to vibrant life the long-forgotten story of Isaac Brown, a hunted fugitive slave and family man whose battle for freedom brought international attention to the injustices of an unbridled slave power. The husband of a free woman and the father of their eleven children, Brown's sudden arrest for the attempted murder of his master — a crime he did not commit — his sale to New Orleans, his escape and later capture in Philadelphia, drew the ire of Pennsylvania's anti-slavery vanguard.

"Marshalling the support of some of the most powerful abolitionists and brilliant legal minds in the United States at the time, Brown was cunningly liberated and secretly whisked to freedom in Canada. Constantly vigilant against the possibility that the long reach of his master and the pro-slavery governor of Maryland, determined to seek his re-enslavement, would find him, Brown changed his name to Russell and struggled to support his family. Drifting into obscurity in his later years, the legacy of Brown and his family's pursuit of liberty and self-determination in the face of extreme opposition is an inspiration and a reminder of the struggles of those who came before us, and whose memory we should never forget."

— **Kate Clifford Larson**, Ph.D., author of *Bound for the Promised Land: Harriet Tubman, Portrait of an American Hero* and *The Assassin's Accomplice: Mary Surratt and the Plot to Kill Abraham Lincoln*

"This heart-rending story of Isaac Brown's separation from family through the horrors and tribulations of slavery and his reunion with his wife, Susannah, follows their odyssey on the Underground Railroad.... Bryan Prince takes us through a personal discovery of the struggle for freedom and dignity of his own ancestors and their eventual settlement in Buxton."

— **Paul Lovejoy**, Fellow of the Royal Society of Canada and director of Harriet Tubman Institute, York University

One More
River to Cross

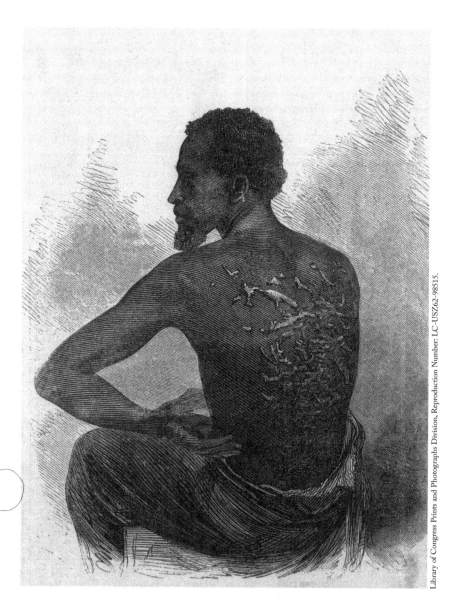

This sketch of a man identified only as "Gordon" shows how the painful reminders of the lash permanently disfigured the backs of slaves like Isaac Brown. Sketch is from Harper's Weekly, *July 4, 1863, which attributes the original photo to McPherson and Oliver.*

One More River to Cross

BRYAN PRINCE

DUNDURN
NATURAL HERITAGE
TORONTO

Editor: Jane Gibson
Copy-editor: Shannon Whibbs
Design: Jennifer Scott
Printer: Webcom

Library and Archives Canada Cataloguing in Publication

Prince, Bryan, 1951-
    One more river to cross / by Bryan Prince.

Includes bibliographical references and index.
Issued also in electronic formats.
ISBN 978-1-4597-0153-3

1. Brown, Isaac, slave. 2. Slaves--United States--Biography. 3. Fugitive slaves--United States--Biography. 4. Fugitive slaves--Canada--History--19th century. 5. Underground Railroad. I. Title.

E450.P75 2012   973.7'115092   C2011-903788-2

1   2   3   4   5   16   15   14   13   12

We acknowledge the support of the **Canada Council for the Arts** and the **Ontario Arts Council** for our publishing program. We also acknowledge the financial support of the **Government of Canada** through the **Canada Book Fund** and **Livres Canada Books**, and the **Government of Ontario** through the **Ontario Book Publishing Tax Credit** and the **Ontario Media Development Corporation**.

Care has been taken to trace the ownership of copyright material used in this book. The author and the publisher welcome any information enabling them to rectify any references or credits in subsequent editions.

J. Kirk Howard, President

Printed and bound in Canada.
www.dundurn.com

Cover images:
Front Cover: Slave Hunt, Dismal Swamp, Virginia, 1862, Thomas Moran, artist. Gift of Laura A. Clubb, 1947.8.44. Courtesy of Philbrook Museum of Art, Inc., Tulsa, Oklahoma
Back Cover: This scene, sometime between 1900 and 1920, shows the backbreaking work involved in harvesting sugar cane. Little had changed in the decades following Isaac Brown's brief enslavement on the sugar plantation of William Kenner. Image from Library of Congress Print and Photographs Division, Reproduction Number: LC-D41-13. Published here courtesy of copyright holder Milwaukee Public Museum, negative #7498.

Dundurn	Gazelle Book Services Limited	Dundurn
3 Church Street, Suite 500	White Cross Mills	2250 Military Road
Toronto, Ontario, Canada	High Town, Lancaster, England	Tonawanda, NY
M5E 1M2	LA1 4XS	U.S.A. 14150

Well, I have gazed for the first time upon Free Land, and, would you believe it, tears sprang to my eyes, and I wept. Oh, it was a glorious sight to gaze for the first time on a land where a poor slave flying from our glorious land of liberty would in a moment find his fetters broken, his shackles loosed, and whatever he was in the land of Washington, beneath the shadow of Bunker Hill Monument or even Plymouth Rock, here he becomes a man and a brother. I have gazed on Harper's Ferry, or rather the rock at the Ferry; I have seen it towering up in simple grandeur, with the gentle Potomac gliding peacefully at its feet, and felt that that was God's masonry, and my soul had expanded in gazing on its sublimity. I have seen the ocean singing its wild chorus of sounding waves, and ecstasy has thrilled upon the living chords of my heart. I have since then seen the rainbow-crowned Niagara chanting the choral hymn of Omnipotence, girdled with grandeur, and robed with glory; but none of these things have melted me as the first sight of Free Land.[1]

— FRANCES ELLEN WATKINS,
September 12, 1856

In memory of Isaac and Susannah

Contents

Preface

Although the murder had occurred fourteen long years ago, Isaac still replayed the scene a thousand times in his head. The passage of time had made it no less criminal or incredible. After all, his older brother's transgression had been so minor, so forgivable, so human. He had simply asked their master's permission to marry the girl who could bring some joy to his life and make his existence a little more bearable. Never mind that they could not live together, residing as she did on another plantation, and, in the eyes of the law, belonged to someone else. Both his master and hers had the power to levy out small favours in small doses and to withdraw them at their pleasure.

The wedding had gone ahead as planned. Alexander Somerville had allowed Isaac's brother to make the short trip on a Sunday to take a bride. The ceremony was probably nothing elaborate — perhaps as simple as the African tradition of one of the elder slave women granting her blessing to the union and telling the young couple to jump the broom into the land of matrimony. Her words would have admonished them to thwart bad omens by taking care not to allow any piece of their garments to touch the broom as they leaped. Although stripped bare of the pomp and circumstance that the nuptials of the master class would have displayed, this marriage would have the same reverence in the minds of the participants as if it had been held in any of the grand cathedrals of Europe. The silent prayer of those in attendance would have been that none of the children that the couple might be blessed with in the future would be sold away from their parents and that one day all might be together and free.

But all of those entreaties were dramatically obliterated when Isaac's brother failed to return home for Monday morning chores by the time appointed by his owner. Demanding to know the reason, the brother replied that he had overslept. Somerville's smouldering anger evolved into broiling rage accompanied by the thrust of a dagger to the side, and the victim's life streamed away into pools of red on the ground.[2] Now, years later, Isaac's blood also flowed freely, but this time following each strike of the jailor's lash that ripped apart the flesh on his back.

Ninety-seven...

Ninety-eight...

Ninety-nine....

Chapter One

God Is Going to Trouble the Waters

Wade in the water
Wade in the water, children
Wade in the water
God is going to trouble the waters.

— Traditional

Thus far it was an uneventful autumn evening on the grounds of Alexander Somerville in Calvert County, Maryland. By Isaac Brown's account, he was with his family at his own home, three miles distant from the home of his master. He was considered to be quiet and loyal, so much so that he had been given the supervision of his owner's more remote plantation on which he lived. Although of the average height at five feet eight inches, he was powerfully built and his physical presence as well as his temperament had made him an ideal candidate for his position. Married to Susannah, a free woman, and the father of eleven children — all free because they assumed the status of their mother — he had outwardly appeared to be content with his lot. He was a part of a much larger black community whose member's occupations were farmers, carpenters, mechanics, servants, sailors, fishermen, and oystermen who plied the waters of the Atlantic Ocean, the Patuxent River and Chesapeake Bay. In the immediate district of Calvert County in which he lived, the number of slaves and free persons was almost equal. When the roughly three hundred free blacks were added to the number of slaves, the blacks outnumbered the whites.[1]

It was a beautiful, natural setting — rolling hills, small ravines, and tall forests. Tobacco, the king crop of the area, was grown on the flatter plateaus. Along the coast of the Chesapeake, beautiful beaches and high cliffs offered an impressive view of Maryland's distant Eastern Shore.

The lord of the lands had much to enjoy in his domestic and business life. Somerville's family had come a long way since his earliest ancestor arrived in the New World more than a century earlier. He was sent as a prisoner to be sold as an "indentured servant," exiled from his native Scotland for taking up arms to attempt to return the Stuarts to the British throne.[2] The generations of the family had prospered in the ensuing years, acquiring wealth, property, and an elevated status in the county. Alexander continued to build upon that familial foundation. In 1840, five free blacks lived on his farm: three children and two adult women, who would have served as domestic servants. Another white couple also lived on the premises, presumably the overseer and his wife. Along with them were thirty-three slaves of both sexes and a wide range of ages. Most of them worked on their owner's farms, however, two worked on vessels in the nearby waterways. Within a decade despite the departure of some by sale or by death, the number of slaves would nearly double.[3]

Somerville's wife, Cornelia Olivia Sewell — commonly referred to as Olivia — had a very interesting family history of her own. Her mother's family, who were of Swiss heritage and Mennonite faith, were among the earliest settlers of Lancaster County, Pennsylvania. When Olivia's parents were married, her father, Charles Sewell, moved from his home in Maryland to his bride's house in Pennsylvania, bringing several slaves with him. According to terms of Pennsylvania's 1780 Act for the Gradual Abolition of Slavery "persons passing through or sojourning in this State" could retain their slaves no longer than six months.[4] Sewell followed the example of many others by returning to Maryland with his slaves for a few minutes each time the six-month anniversary approached, technically allowing him to retain his chattels *ad infinitum*. Once the state legislature tightened up that loophole by amending the Act in 1788, Sewell manumitted at least two of his slaves *with* the stipulation that they become "indentured servants" and serve him for another seven years. Sewell also attempted to evade the spirit of another term of the Act by registering the infant children of these "indentured servants" as slaves until the age of twenty-eight.[5]

These subterfuges were noticed by William Wright, an anti-slavery activist who belonged to the Society of Friends. Wright carefully charted the elapse of time between Sewell's visits to Maryland and immediately initiated a court case to have the slaves declared free when their master missed a six-month deadline. Sewell was enraged when the court freed his property and chased Wright at full gallop, occasionally striking the fleeing Quaker with a rawhide whip. However, no amount of physical retribution could reverse the ruling of the court and the disgusted Sewell soon sold his wife's land in Pennsylvania, packed up their belongings, and returned to Maryland to raise Olivia and his other children in a state where no such anti-slavery laws existed.[6]

By October 23, 1845, Olivia and Alexander Somerville were soon to celebrate their thirteenth wedding anniversary, which would take place on the sixth of the following month. Their young family was growing — Charles, their eldest, was twelve, Mary Elizabeth was nine, and Alexander Jr. was a toddler of two. With supper finished, most of the family was in another part of the house. As the shadows grew longer at the end of the day while his servant girl cleaned the supper dishes from the table and his daughter Mary played on the living room floor, Somerville reached for the newspaper and settled into his chair to relax and catch up with the happenings beyond the confines of his family farm. His interests were varied, having served as a county representative to plan a grand commemoration of the landing of first Europeans on the shores of Maryland, a trustee to establish an academy in the neighbouring town of Prince Frederick, and a vice-president of the state's temperance society. Although it is unclear if he did so from motives of benevolence to give them a homeland of their own or if it was to remove those whose liberty served as a disruption to the minds of the enslaved, he had even pledged money to the Maryland State Colonization Society to assist in building a vessel to send free blacks to a colony in Liberia.[7] The newspapers carried many regular advertisements as well as stories from a variety of sources from across the country and occasionally across the ocean.

Isaac Brown's mistress, Cornelia Olivia Sewell Somerville, and his master, Alexander Somerville, were leading citizens in Calvert County. According to the Baltimore Sun *of February 7, 1845, the governor of Maryland had appointed Alexander to the Orphans' Court, which settled wills and estates, including the appointment of guardians for minor children. He also had once been a Whig candidate for the State Legislature. From* A History of the Kägy Relationship in America from 1715 to 1900, *(1899).*

With his attention focused on the open pages before him, Somerville did not notice the barrel of the gun that silently slid onto the sill of the open window. The gun was loaded with large squirrel shot that was designed to bring down small game, but was potentially lethal to much larger prey. Without warning, the trigger was pulled and the newspaper instantly shredded in his hands. As it was intended to do, the squirrel shot scattered, striking its target in the shoulder, neck, roots of the tongue, and side of the head. The wounds were extensive and severe and the doctors who were immediately summoned had little hope that Somerville could survive.[8]

The overseer was quickly summoned, but as he approached the house he reported that he heard the firing of another gun, and, fearing that he was the intended mark, dove for cover, thereby missing the opportunity to see the shooter. When the panic finally subsided somewhat, the overseer entered the main house. When his employer was able to gather the strength to whisper, he instructed the overseer to go to Isaac Brown's house to ascertain if that slave was at home. Although he had not seen the gunman, he had the suspicion that it may have been Brown. Still shaken and fearful of his own safety, the overseer sheepishly declined to do as he was bid.[9]

Word of the attack rapidly spread throughout the rural neighbourhood. Rumours of slave uprisings and violent mutinous retributions frequently caused waves of uneasiness among whites throughout the South. Before long, an armed posse assembled to track down the culprit and to apply swift judgment. It was not reported if there was any recent cause to conclude Brown's guilt, but Somerville was very much aware that he had reneged on his promise to give Brown his freedom upon reaching the age of thirty-five. And, of course, it would have been common knowledge that Somerville had taken the life of Brown's brother and had neither been arrested nor tried for his crime. According to the law, blacks who may have watched the stabbing were not allowed to testify and there were no white witnesses. Somerville had effortlessly gotten away with murder. Now, the evolving pervasive thought was that, although it was a dish served cold, Brown had finally taken his revenge.

Isaac Brown gave a very different account. He swore that he was innocent of the charge and that he was, as others could confirm, at his

MELANCHOLY AFFAIR.—We regret to learn that Mr. Alexander Somerville, of Calvert county, Md., was shot on Thursday night last, and very dangerously, if not fatally, wounded. Mr. S. was sitting in his own room, at the time, reading a newspaper. The gun was fired through the window, and a large number of shot lodged in his face, neck and shoulder. Physicians were immediately called in and the wounds dressed; but very slight hopes were entertained of his recovery on the following day. One of Mr. Somerville's servants has been arrested on suspicion of having perpetrated the bloody act.—*Baltimore Patriot of Monday evening.*

The notice of the assault on Alexander Somerville was widely reprinted in several parts of the country, including the one shown here, printed in the Baltimore Sun *on October 29, 1845.*

home. It was only upon hearing of the shooting that he quickly left his house, jumped onto his horse, and made haste to his master's dwelling. While en route, he met with a group of armed men who took him into custody and carried him to the county jail at Prince Frederick.

Newspapers from around the country rushed to print the sensationalized story. Readers of *The Baltimore Patriot, The Boston Daily Patriot, The New York Herald,* and Gettysburg's *Star and Republican Banner* were among those shocked by the details. Even the premier national anti-slavery newspaper of the day, the *Liberator,* reprinted the story under the heading ASSASSINATION. The November 1, 1845, edition of the *Maryland Republican* from Annapolis reported: "The circumstances, as related to us, are very strong, and will, no doubt, be sufficient to convict him." It appeared that Isaac Brown's guilt had already been determined.

Chapter Two

And We Became Desperate

We were thrust into the hold of the vessel in a state of nudity, the males being crammed on one side and the females on the other; the hold was so low that we were obliged to crouch; day and night were the same to us sleep being denied as from the confined position of our bodies, and we became desperate through suffering and fatigue ....[1]

— Mahommah Gardo Baquaqua,
Chatham, Canada West, 1845

The nightmare for the accused only became more vivid and painful as the minutes ticked by in the county jail. Hours turned into days until the entire month of November passed and December began. Despite his and his family's protestations to the contrary and a total lack of evidence against him, Brown was not only imprisoned, but also tortured. On two different occasions, each within a week of the other, all of his clothing was removed, his hands and feet were bound together, and he was flogged with a cow-skin whip by the jailer, Sandy Buck. It was one hundred lashes to his naked body each time. Still, Brown denied the charges. To further add to his torment, Brown's daughter, Lucinda, was arrested and placed into jail with her father. The vengeful authorities hoped that she could be induced to implicate him in the attempted murder. But she remained steadfast in her story that her father was entirely innocent and had been with her, three miles away, when the offence was committed. Her anguished mother, Susannah, made the same plea.[2]

Thirty-three days passed and still there was no evidence brought forward to substantiate the charges. In the absence of any legal foundation, Somerville decided to proceed with what was arguably the ultimate penalty — permanent separation of Brown from his family and banishment from the state of Maryland to the Deep South. Lucinda Brown heard that this sentence was carried out with the consent or advice of Governor Thomas G. Pratt.[3] At the time, the governor was wrestling in his own mind with the subject of proper punishment for slaves. By law, slaves convicted of serious crimes were not to be confined in the penitentiary, but could be whipped or sold out of state, whereas free persons of any race would be incarcerated for anywhere between two and twenty years. Pratt found this inconsistency appalling and felt that selling a slave into another state "would neither be considered by the slave or the community as any punishment whatever."[4] Isaac, Susannah, Lucinda, and all of the Brown's family and loved ones would disagree.

The widespread news of Brown's case drew the attention of the Maryland slave traders who frequented the area jails, watching for deals to purchase runaways, blacks who were convicted of crimes, or for those who had been placed there "for safekeeping," (which was often the code word for being held before they were sold South). Two such traders, Thomas Wilson and Samuel Y. Harris (a.k.a. Hickman Harris), visited the Prince Frederick jail to appraise the prisoner within. Both had ties to the largest of all the Maryland traders: Hope Hull Slatter, who headquartered his business in Baltimore and New Orleans. Wilson was in fact Slatter's agent.[5] Harris, who lived in Upper Marlboro, had his own business and travelled the countryside looking for product to stock his own pen, promising to "take any number of negroes" and "give the highest market price in cash."[6] Fudging slightly on the last point, Harris made the deal for Brown for $500 and in turn sold Brown to Hope Slatter for $665 — pocketing a quick and substantial profit in a few days' time.[7]

The eighty-five-mile trip from Prince Frederick to Baltimore must have been excruciating for Brown. Pain came in many guises. The effects from the whippings and other terrors of his recent past were still fresh on his body and in his mind and would accompany him for a lifetime. Even more acute was the dread associated with

the uncertainty for what the future might hold. Chances of ever seeing his family again were remote. Hope Hull Slatter was feared and
hated by blacks across the country. Much had been spoken and written about him. He was raised in Georgia and, after borrowing $4,000
from his mother, moved to Baltimore and began his rapid rise to the
top of the slave-trading ranks. Someone who knew him observed that
although Slatter was very polite and took a special pride "on his good
morals and genteel manners," he was detested by most people in the
city. Those facts were confirmed by Joseph Sturge, the founder of the
British and Foreign Anti-Slavery Society. When the two men met,
Sturge felt that Slatter was very courteous and was further gratified by
the slave-trader's assurances that he never parted families. Even more
stunning was Slatter's claim that his reputation for kindness among
blacks was so admired that he was often asked by slaves if he would
purchase them. He even left his slave pen in the care of a head slave for
weeks at a time. Further suggesting his eligibility for sainthood, Slatter
guaranteed his deeply devout Quaker guest that he had never swore
"nor committed an immoral act in his life." Clearly impressed, Sturge,
in later correspondence, made the Freudian slip of spelling the slave
trader's name as Hope H. *Slaughter*.[8] Joshua Giddings, the United
States congressman from Ohio, labelled Slatter as "a fiend in human
shape."[9] A more picturesque image, with no admiration intended, was
given by the Underground Railroad martyr, Charles T. Torrey, who
declared that "Slatter looks like Raphael's picture of Judas Iscariot."[10]

According to advertisements in the *Baltimore Sun* and elsewhere,
including Sturge's description, Slatter took pains to establish an impressive business. Many other newspapers from various states, as well as in
England, carried the ad as a cautionary tale. The *British Emancipator*
called it "the most shameful and horrible advertisements of those slave-
dealers and traffickers in human flesh, who are making our country a
hissing and by-word among the nations, and calling down upon us the
vengeance of a just and holy God … Horrible! Most Horrible."[11]

Isaac Brown and his fellow inmates, who shared the two-storey
brick building with barred windows, would not have found the accommodations as opulent and comfortable as described. Appearances were

Hope Hull Slatter ran advertisements in several newspapers, including the Baltimore Sun *for many years in the 1830s and 1840s. Abolitionist newspapers such as the* Liberator (Boston) *also frequently carried articles such as this one that appeared in its Friday, February 24, 1843, issue 8 edition, page 30.*

CASH FOR NEGROES.
The highest prices will, at all times, be given for NEGROES OF BOTH SEXES, that are slaves for life and good titles. My office is in *Pratt-st. No.* 85, *between Sharp and Howard-streets,* where myself or my agent, J. M. Wilson, can be seen at all times. All persons having negroes to sell would do well to see me before they dispose of them, as I am always buying and forwarding to the New-Orleans market. I will also receive and keep negroes at twenty five cents each day, and forward them to any southern port, at the request of the owner. My establishment is large, comfortable and airy, and all above ground, and kept in complete order, with a large yard for exercise, and is the strongest and most splendid building of the kind in the United States. And, as the character of my house and yard is so completely established, for strength, comfort and cleanliness, and it being a place where I keep all my own, that I will not be accountable, for the future, for escapes of any kind from my establishment.
HOPE H. SLATTER.
Baltimore, Aug. 20, 1842.
 1y

important to Slatter and he allowed his stock to play cards or dance to fiddle or banjo music. Some visitors were treated to athletic exhibitions where the prisoners were taught to display "their power, their health, their ambition and their spirit, so they would be purchased in all confidence as contented, happy servants." Slatter's staff would roll up their sleeves to show their muscled arms. Occasionally, appreciative or sympathetic onlookers would throw pennies to them through the tall stockade gate. There was an enclosed courtyard, approximately twenty-five square feet, where the inmates where allowed to spend the daylight hours. However, all was not as benign as appeared on the surface. The brick walls surrounding the yard were about twenty feet high, and a large and ferocious bloodhound helped to serve as a sentry. One who had spent time within those walls had the duty of preparing other slaves for sale by greasing their bodies as to enhance the appearance of their physiques. Both male and females were often stripped naked and tied face-down on a bench and held down by two or four men and strapped with a leather strap rather than a cowhide whip so as not to cut into the flesh.[12]

Isaac Brown's stay within the pen was short-lived as a shipment of slaves was due to depart within days of his arrival. A northern newspaper reported first-hand observations of a group of slaves who were removed from Slatter's pen and loaded onto a train car, soon to be loaded onto a ship destined for the Deep South:

> About half of them were females, a few of whom had but a slight tinge of African blood in their veins, and were finely formed and beautiful. The men were ironed together, and the whole group looked sad and dejected.... In the middle of the car stood the notorious slave-dealer of Baltimore, Slatter.... He had purchased the men and women around him and was taking his departure ... this old, grey-headed villain, — this dealer in the bodies and souls of men ...
>
> Some of the colored people ... were weeping most bitterly. Wives were there to take leave of their husbands, and husbands of their wives, children of their parents, brothers and sisters shaking hands perhaps for the last time, friends parting with friends, and the tenderest ties of humanity sundered at the single bid of the inhuman slave-broker before them.[13]

It is not recorded if Isaac Brown had a similar heart-wrenching parting with his loved ones, who remained at his former home in Calvert County, many miles away. Perhaps their goodbyes were exchanged at the Prince Frederick jail. To help ensure that he remained in control, Slatter generally loaded his human cargo onto a train of omnibuses and followed the procession to the wharf on horseback, "callous to the wailings" about him.[14] We are left to wonder if the two traders who had first inspected Isaac Brown in the Prince Frederick jail, Thomas Wilson and Samuel Harris, were Slatter's agents at that scene who were described as "two ruffianly-looking personages, with large canes in their hands, and, if their countenances were an index of their hearts, they were the very impersonation of hardened villany itself." One of these men, who knocked a husband down as he tried to say farewell to his wife, was

Slaves bound for southern destinations from Hope Hull Slater's pen in Baltimore were transported under cover of darkness to awaiting ships by a horse-drawn omnibus, such as the one pictured above. In Five Hundred Thousand Strokes for Freedom: A Series of Anti-Slavery Tracts, *Wilson Armistead reprinted the observations of an unidentified British traveller that had originally been printed in the Leeds Anti-slavery Series, No. 9, which related a touching scene: "I saw a young man who kept pace with the carriages, that he might catch one more glimpse of a dear friend, before she was torn forever from his sight. As she saw him, she burst into a flood of tears, and was hurried out of his sight, sorrowing most of all that they should see each others' faces no more."*

further described as "a monster more hideous, hardened and savage, than the blackest spirit of the pit."[15]

On December 17, 1845, Isaac Brown was placed on board the two-masted ship *Victorine* at Wilson's wharf at the Baltimore Harbor along with eighty-two others. The *Victorine* regularly made the circuit from New Orleans to Baltimore with occasional stops to load or unload shipments at Norfolk and Richmond, Virginia, or Charleston, South Carolina, and at more northerly ports such as New York City. The vessel was described as being "the very fast sailing packet brig ... having elegant accommodations."[16] What the advertisement did not make clear was that those "elegant accommodations" were reserved for the very few paying southbound passengers who were comfortable enough to book passage on a domestic slaver. Travellers from New Orleans to more northerly ports were more likely to purchase a ticket knowing that the cargo consisted of such inanimate goods as bags of corn or wheat, bales of cotton and hemp, and barrels of pork, lard, and molasses.

Brown and his fellow sufferers replaced that merchandise in the hold for the coastal voyage.[17] Joining them were fifteen other slaves belonging to other area dealers, Joseph Donovan and Bernard Campbell.[18] While the slaves were trying to grasp the reality of what was about to befall them, Hope Slatter signed the necessary documents with the port authority. He provided a list of all of the names, ages, and heights. They were further described by their colour: black, brown, or yellow. Most of the thirty-nine men were in their twenties. There were eighteen people in their teens and twenty aged twelve and under — twelve of whom were listed as "infants." There were forty-three females, many of them mother and child. It is particularly poignant to read the names of the many members of the Haley family — fifteen in all whose ages ranged from thirty-eight for Larry to two years for John. We are left to wonder what the circumstances were for all of them to be sold. At least in this case, Slatter appeared to be true to his word not to separate families. But what New Orleans buyer would have either the financial means or the inclination to make such a large purchase to keep them together?

Isaac Brown was listed as black, five feet eight inches tall, and thirty years old. Slatter fudged Brown's age by many years as he was actually in his mid-forties, and, except for one person listed as fifty-one, older than everyone else in the shipment. This was probably the early stages of his plan to make Brown more attractive to prospective buyers. The still unhealed stripes across his back would make most shoppers shy away from expressing any interest as it was believed that slaves who had evidence of whippings were headstrong, unmanageable, and bound to be more trouble than they were worth. Volunteering his true age would only compound the challenge. To reinforce the illusion of youth, a common tactic in the trade was to meticulously pull out any grey hairs, or, if there was too much, dye it all.[19]

Before the *Victorine* could be cleared to disembark, both Slatter and the ship's captain had to sign the manifest for Richard Snowden, the

National Archives Records Administration, Washington, D.C., Record Group 36, U.S. Customs Service Records, Port of New Orleans, Louisiana, Inward Slave Manifests 1846, microfilm roll 16, 1846–47, image 19.

The image shown is an Inward Slave manifest to port of New Orleans. Isaac Brown appears as no. 7 on the list. Note that there are two young women with the surname Brown — no. 43 and no. 44 — Mary Ann, age fifteen; and Elizabeth, age fourteen. There is no evidence to suggest that they may have been related to Isaac. These manifests are also available online from www.ancestry.com.

inspector of the customs house, to swear that the dealings were legal and did not contravene the United States abolition of the transatlantic slave trade that had taken place thirty-seven years earlier. At 10:00 o'clock, the principals put their signatures to the document:

> District of Baltimore, — Port of Baltimore,
> Hope H. Slatter owner & shipper of the persons named, and particularly describe in the above manifest of slaves and James T. Forrest, Master of the Brig Victorine do solemnly, sincerely, and truly swear, each of us to the best of our knowledge and belief that the above slaves have not been imported into the United States since the first day of January, one thousand eight hundred and eight; and that under the Laws of the State of Maryland are held to service or labor as slaves and are not entitled to freedom under these.
> Sworn to this 17th day of December 1845.
> Hope H. Slatter
> James T. Forrest[20]

The weather had been particularly harsh as the *Victorine* attempted to leave the harbour. The steamer *Relief*, a specially designed "ice boat"

For Baltimore—Orleans Line.—The very fast sailing packet brig VICTORINE, Capt. J. F. Forrest, having the principal part of her cargo engaged, will have quick despatch. For balance of freight, or passage, having elegant accommodations, apply to the captain on board, opposite the Beef Market, or to   C. J. MEEKER, 66 Poydras street. The V. will take freight for Norfolk and Richmond, with privilege of reshipment at Baltimore.   s30

After depositing its cargo of slaves in New Orleans, the owners of the Victorine *advertised in* The Daily Picayune *(New Orleans), January 10, 1846, for freight and passengers for the return trip to Baltimore.*

that was employed to cut through the frozen ice of the Chesapeake Bay, towed them out to open water.[21] There had been gale-force winds the previous day and heavy snows surrounded them, most particularly to the south. The knowledge that ships had been battered and damaged in the storms and heavy seas of that week added to the feelings of dread and the confinement, and the crowding and the discomfort did nothing to help the cargo find their sea legs. As they sailed into an unknown future and into the Christmas season, those hanging precariously to their faith must have questioned how God could have so unmercifully forsaken them. Although probably locked away in the cargo hold to prevent escape, Isaac Brown would have gazed with his mind's eye upon the familiar coast of Calvert County and the faces of his loved ones as the ship passed by his home. He had no way of knowing that his former master, Alexander Somerville, who was recovering from his wounds, had confided to Susannah Brown that upon reflection he no longer believed that Isaac had shot him and regretted having sold her husband whom he always considered to be "a peaceable and quiet man, and had done everything he wanted him to do."[22]

Chapter Three

Give Me Liberty

The night is dark, and keen the air,
And the Slave is flying to be free;
His parting word is one short prayer;
O God, but give me Liberty!
Farewell — farewell;
Behind I leave the whips and chains,
Before me spreads sweet Freedom's plains.[1]

— From *The-Anti-Slavery-Harp*

As the New Year dawned, the *Victorine* entered the Gulf of Mexico after rounding the tip of Florida, sailed past southernmost Alabama, and approached the coast of Louisiana. On Friday, January 2, 1846, favourable weather accompanied its arrival after a voyage of two weeks.[2] Isaac Brown and his comrades were probably allowed to come up onto the deck during certain times during the day for fresh air and exercise beneath the billowing sails before being locked away into the hold at night. It was a critical order of business that the slaves be as well fed and fit as possible so as to demand the highest price for would-be buyers once they reached their destination. It was also good for morale to be released from the crowded conditions made worse by crying infants and the overpowering odours that assaulted the senses.

An increasing feeling of apprehension would have overwhelmed Isaac Brown as all on board awaited the rumbling steamboat *Hercules* to tow the sailing ship against the current into the mouth of the Mississippi and to navigate the 110 miles up to the dock. The various New Orleans newspapers that faithfully recorded details of the many vessels' arrivals, departures, passenger lists, and cargo printed only that the *Victorine* imported "assorted mdze" and a sole passenger, "Mr. Skipwith." Although the identity of Brown and the others on board were not deemed worthy to print, the customs officer reviewed their names and physical descriptions on the second copy of the ship manifest that Hope Slatter had signed in Baltimore. The officer signed his name with an indecipherable flourish, confirming that there were ninety-five slaves on board, two less than had originally boarded. No explanation for the discrepancy was recorded, but they presumably had fallen fatal victims to illness and despair and were laid to rest in a watery Atlantic grave.

New Orleans, the fourth-largest city in the United States, was a vital cosmopolitan centre. Native Americans and Creoles, who were descended from the early French settlers, interacted with English, Irish, Germans, and Spaniards. Upon arrival, Brown would have been amazed at the cacophony of different languages being spoken everywhere. Porters and people selling newspapers, books, candy, and fruit, along with stevedores unloading ships of cotton, whisky barrels, food stuffs, and other cargo filled the mile-long levee that served as the wharf. People of African descent were omnipresent.

A visitor to New Orleans described the city as full of open depravity — gambling, drinking, cock-fights, infidelity, theatre, circuses, the worship of money, horse racing, miscegenation, duelling, and an irreverent disregard for the Sabbath. With almost child-like wonder at the dichotomy that surrounded him, the visitor went on to conclude:

> The truth is New Orleans appears to me to be at the extreme of everything, the hottest, the dirtiest, the most sickly, and at times the most healthy, the busiest and the most dull, the most wicked & the most orderly. They have in truth the most business, the best of land, the prettiest of women, the fastest of horses and the most delightful climate. It rains harder, it is more dusty. It is hotter and has a more diversified people than any city

in the union. Changes take place here with almost the rapidity of thought. Today rich, tomorrow poor, today well, tomorrow dead, today hot, tomorrow cold, today dry, tomorrow wet, suffocating for air one day and the next suffering from extreme winds which almost view with a hurricane in their fierceness. You see here some of the richest & some of the poorest of humanity.[3]

He described the blacks as "a bundle of oddities, of strange conceits and singular notions" with a love for "high flown words and his aping the manners of the whites." He differentiated between the free and enslaved by noting "then there is your plantation nigger, of an entirely different species, coarser, poorer dressed and an entirely different dialect." He placed blacks into several different categories and viciously ridiculed them all, with the exception of the beautiful quadroon women, whom he pitied.[4]

This panoramic "Bird's Eye View of New Orleans" and the Mississippi River depicts a scene similar to that of the Victorine *being towed into port by the steamboat* Hercules. *The original was drawn by J. Bachman in 1851.*

Brown would have little opportunity or inclination to absorb all of those surroundings as he, chained together with his fellows, was herded through the streets. His first impression may have been like that of another slave "If there is anything like a hell on earth, New Orleans must be the place."[5] The forced march and the introduction to Hope Slatter's slave pen at the corner of Moreau and Esplanade streets in New Orleans' famous "French Quarter" was bewildering. Slatter's son Henry, his brother Shadrack, and his agent James T. Blakeny ran the southern branch of the family business. Shadrack had once boasted to an abolitionist visitor to the Baltimore slave pen that "I treat my niggers in the kindest manner. When they arrive at the South, I give them pleasant homes, and every one is furnished with a good bed, and a net to keep off the musquetoes! Why, d---n it, there is not a happier set of laborers on God's earth than the niggers of the South"[6]

The traders took deliberate measures to ensure that the slaves did not fail in presenting themselves as being happy with their lot in life, as one of the condemned described:

> As the importance of "looking bright" under such circumstances may not be readily understood by the ordinary run of readers, I may as well explain that the price a slave fetches depends, in a great measure, upon the general appearance he or she presents to the intending buyer. A man or a woman may be well made, and physically faultless in every respect, yet their value be impaired by a sour look, or a dull, vacant stare, or a general dullness of demeanour. For this reason the poor wretches who are about to be sold, are instructed to look "spry and smart": to hold themselves well up, and put on a smiling, cheerful countenance. They are also told to speak up for, and recommend themselves; to conceal any defects they may have, and especially not to tell their age when they are getting past the active period of life. It is quite a truism that "a nigger never knows when he was born," for though he may be quite certain of the year, and might

swear to it blindfold, he must say he is just as old as his master chooses to bid him do, or he will have to take the consequences. It may be conceived that "nigger trading" is as much a calling as any other, and that there is an enormous amount of cheating and roguery in it. There are "nigger jockeys" as well as horse jockeys, and as many tricks are played off to sell a bad or an unsound "nigger," as there are to palm off a diseased horse; and the man who succeeds in "shoving off a used up nigger," as one sound in wind and limb, takes as much pride in boasting of it, as the horse dealer does who has taken in a green-horn with a wall-eyed pony. Of course these "tricks of the trade" are known, and every means are employed to defeat attempts at dishonest sales. I dare not —for decency's sake — detail the various expedients that are resorted to by dealers to test the soundness of a male or a female slave. When I say that they are handled in the grossest manner, and inspected with the most elaborate and disgusting minuteness, I have said enough for the most obtuse understanding to fill up the outline of the horrible picture. What passes behind the screen in the auction-room, or in the room where the dealer is left alone with the "chattels" offered to him to buy, only those who have gone through the ordeal can tell. But God has recorded the wickedness that is done there, and punish-ment will assuredly fall upon the guilty.[7]

On the same day as Isaac Brown and his fellow sufferer's arrival, and for weeks later, an advertisement ran in *Le Courier de la Louisiane* that Slatter was offering one hundred slaves for sale — sixty of whom were from one plantation and without doubt included the aforemen-tioned Haley family — made up of field hands, house servants, wash-ers, cooks, ironers, mechanics from Virginia and Maryland, and will continue to receive more as he had for the past twelve years. The slaves would be fully guaranteed against defects. The clichéd salesman's

According to historian Walter Johnson, author of Soul by Soul: Life Inside the Antebellum Slave Market, *this 1866 watercolour of buildings at the corner of Esplanade and Chartres Streets in New Orleans was once the slave pen of Hope H. Slatter.*

pledge concluded the ad: "Will be sold low."[8] To ensure that the advertisement reached the largest possible audience, it was also printed in French under the title: NEGRES À VENDRE. CENT NEGRES DE LA VIRGINIE ET DU MARYLAND.

In January 1846, the Slatters sold Brown to forty-five-year-old William Butler Kenner, who had made the trip of sixteen miles to the markets of New Orleans to shop for several more male slaves needed to work his land, which stretched from the Mississippi River to Lake Pontchartrain. He employed over one hundred slaves for the labour-intensive task of cultivating sugar cane on his rich alluvial soils on eastern side of the lower Mississippi Valley, christened "the Oakland Plantation."[9] His late father's roots in the area dated back to the turn of the nineteenth century before the time of the 1803 Louisiana Purchase from the French. William was blessed with the prestige and wealth that followed his father's legacy as a member of the territory's legislature, his role in helping to fend off the British in the Battle of New Orleans during the War of 1812, and as a major figure in the lucrative sugar cane business.[10] William's maternal grandfather, Stephen Minor, was the last Spanish governor of the Natchez region of Mississippi.[11] Building upon his heritage, Kenner and his northern bride, Ruhamah Riske, who descended from illustrious families from Ohio and Pennsylvania, had expanded the family fortunes.[12]

SALE OF ESTATES, PICTURES AND SLAVES IN THE ROTUNDA, NEW ORLEANS.

This image of a sale in New Orleans first appeared as the frontispiece in The Slave States of America *by James Silk Buckingham. The author vividly described the scene that took place in the ornate rotunda of the French Exchange Hotel. Several different auctioneers, each trying to drown out the voices of the others, attempted to sell estate goods, pictures, and an anguished family of slaves.*

But there was a condition placed on the transaction between the Slatters and Kenner before it would be finalized — that the beaten and scarred Isaac Brown must prove that he was productive and manageable during a trial period. This type of deal was not unheard of and Slatter had arranged that sort of business arrangement on other occasions.[13] As one of the largest and most important slave dealers in the country, Hope Slatter and his family had to consider the economic fallout should their reputation for delivering quality hands be tarnished. So much the worse should he disappoint someone of William Butler Kenner's stature. However, Slatter indulged himself in a minor salesman's ploy and resisted any temptation to reveal Brown's true age and clung tightly to the "he is only thirty years old" charade.

Isaac Brown must have marvelled at the incredible riches of the Kenner family. The Oakland plantation was described in the vernacular and measurements of the French who had colonized the area as fronting

Courtesy of State Library of Louisiana, Louisiana Collection. Image ID: hp001880.

This stately mansion on what was known as the Ashland-Belle Helene Plantation in Louisiana showed the tremendous wealth of the Kenner family. It was the home of Duncan F. Kenner, brother of Isaac Brown's owner.

twenty-three arpents (19.55 acres) on the Mississippi.[14] As the slaves approached the farm they would have been dazzled by the magnificent home of Kenner's brother, Minor.

Kenner himself lived in the large old family homestead that was made of hewn cypress logs, made to look even more imposing by being raised in the air to survive the periodic flooding of the river. Several other buildings, including an office, sugar mill, and slave quarters, surrounded the main house.[15]

Brown's new owner regularly travelled north to his wife's home area in Ohio during the oppressive summer season to escape the threat of often fatal maladies such as yellow fever, manifested by creamy eyes, aching bones, colds sweats, and dark phlegm, that regularly descended upon the area. The year previous to acquiring Brown,

Kenner had purchased nine acres on a knoll on the Kentucky side of the Ohio River to build a summer mansion. It is said that he took his domestic slaves with him to wait on his family. Given that, it is little wonder that he chose to build on the slave state side of the river rather than in the neighbouring free state of Ohio where his wife was born. With Cincinnati in clear view, the lure of liberty must have been tremendous for his servants.[16]

RAN AWAY from the plantation of W. B. Kenner, above this city, a negro man named ISAAC BROWN, about thirty years old, 5 feet 10 inches high, and quite stout; he is very black, and may have changed his name, as he absconded without a provication; had a blue suit and other clothing; he is recently from Virginia. m1720* JAMES T. BLAKENY, Moreau st.

The New Orleans Daily Picayune *printed a runaway slave advertisement for Isaac Brown, on March 18, 1846.*

That same lure tugged mightily at Isaac Brown. The beauty of rural Louisiana held no attraction for him as it did for many of thousands of others who by virtue of being free looked upon it with different eyes. Shudders still reverberated throughout the countryside from a failed slave insurrection thirty-five years earlier when two of the Kenner's family's slaves along with sixteen others were sentenced to be taken to Kenner's farm where they were shot, decapitated, and their heads "placed atop a pole in a spot for all to see the punishment meted our for such crimes, also as a terrible example to all who would disturb the public tranquility in the future."[17]

The work that Isaac would be expected to do in growing, harvesting, and processing sugar was exhausting and life expectancy was short. Frederick Douglass, the most prominent black leader of the day and himself a former slave from Maryland, described working in a sugar cane field as "a life of living death" and that escape was nearly impossible.[18]

Even if Brown could somehow flee this sentence and miraculously find his way home, as a runaway slave he could never reunite with his family in Maryland. What good would freedom be to him without his loved ones? At any rate, successful flight seemed impossible. Rivers, mountains, northern snows, uncertainty, and more than a thousand miles of slave territory stood as obstacles between him and freedom. An enraged Hope Hull Slatter, who would forfeit the sale price contracted with William Kenner, had connections to a vast network of slave hunters, patrollers, and trained "negro dogs," and would surely go to great lengths to recoup his losses, and, should the prey be captured, rain down a terrible retribution. But to someone who had already lost everything, what did it matter? The desperate and resourceful husband and father "got very excellently got-up free papers" and took his chances.[19]

Chapter Four

By the Law of Almighty God

*By the law of Almighty God, I was born free — by the law
of man a slave.[1]*

— Aaron Siddles, Chatham, 1855

During the summer of 1846, a quiet stranger calling himself "Samuel
Russell" departed from Pittsburgh in the free northern state of
Pennsylvania and took up residence in Philadelphia. He was stout in stature and appeared to be in his mid-forties. He was guarded about revealing
personal details of his past life. It was not uncommon for runaway slaves
to lose themselves in that city, which had a large black population and a
citizenry with a reputation for possessing strong anti-slavery sentiments.
Numerous benevolent societies as well as a public Alms House that also
housed an Infirmary existed to render aid to the poor and the sick. There
were eighteen black churches — Episcopalian, Presbyterian, Methodist,
and Baptist — scattered across the city to tend to the spiritual needs of
the twenty thousand coloured inhabitants. Several schools, libraries, and
literary societies had been established to encourage education and the
expansion of the mind. Opportunities existed for employment and for
becoming property owners for the able-bodied and the industrious, and
for those who summoned the strength to overcome their private adversi-
ties that possessed a sinister way of removing all hope.[2]

But those aspirations and accomplishments were not automatic for
those who, like Samuel Russell, arrived penniless. He moved into one
of the poorest districts, which was already over-crowded with recent

immigrants. It was common for some of these recent arrivals to sleep outdoors when conditions allowed, and to huddle together in larger groups in shanties when the weather turned against them. The winter of 1846–47 was particularly punishing for them, with freezing temperatures and an epidemic of yellow fever (also known as typhus). Malnutrition and exposure worked in tandem with the fever to send dozens to their graves. Many frozen bodies were found in backyards and alleys or in crude shelters with bare wooden or earthen floors, and with crevices in the walls that allowed the winds to whistle in. Some were asphyxiated from the smoke while huddling around a small coal fire in a stove without a chimney pipe. Many of these were released from a life of begging, stealing, gathering scraps of food discarded from other people's kitchens, or from their miserable occupation collecting and selling rags and bones.[3]

Samuel Russell survived the winter — and whatever hardships he may have experienced in his past. It was hard to guess his status, free man or runaway slave. But he was obviously lonely, despite having developed many friendships in the area. His recent experiences proved to him that some people could be trusted, so he confided his secrets to members of the anti-slavery community, among whom were James and Lucretia Mott, a soft-hearted and quiet Quaker couple who were leaders in that society. James Mott offered Russell a job in his store at 35 Church Alley, which specialized in selling "free produce" dry goods, including cloth made from cotton that had not been picked by slaves. Among the items that they handled were: "Manchester Ginghams," "Canton Flannel," Bird Eye Towels," "black and white Wadding," and "Calicoes," as well as aprons, furniture, lamp wicks, bed ticking, and stockings.[4]

Reuniting the family was viewed as even more important than providing an income for "Russell." Members of the anti-slavery society clandestinely arranged to deliver his wife and nine of their children from Maryland to Philadelphia so they could be with their husband and father. The joy of that meeting can only be imagined. But with two more of their grown-up children remaining in Maryland, there were still vacant spaces in the family circle.

Seeking to fill those empty spaces, Russell took up his pen to compose a letter to his eldest son, addressing it to Calvert County, Maryland.

He wrote his return address — 172 Pine Street, between Fifth and Sixth — and asked the intended recipient of the letter to direct their reply to that address. Before taking the letter to be posted, he made the ill-advised but unavoidable mistake of signing his real name "Isaac Brown."

Trains carried the mails daily from Philadelphia to Baltimore where letters and packages were distributed to the rural postmasters by horse-back or coach.[5] Maryland postmasters were instructed to beware of mail that might have "a tendency to create discontent among and stir up to insurrection, the people of color of this State."[6] While Brown's letter, which was written to reveal his whereabouts to his son and beseech him to join the rest of the family, would not have strictly fallen under those guidelines aimed at abolitionist literature, it was still risky to reveal his true identity. The owners of any prying eyes who had knowledge of Hope Slatter's attempts to retrieve Brown stood to be handsomely rewarded for supplying information as to his whereabouts. Knowing that run-aways would try to get in touch with loved ones made any mail that the younger Browns might receive the subject of close scrutiny.[7]

Somehow the contents of the letter became known to Alexander Somerville. No doubt enraged that he had already lost the services of Susannah Brown and her children who, although free, worked on his farm, Somerville shared the information contained in the letter with Slatter. Determined to recover the $665 purchase price plus the considerable expense he had incurred in housing and shipping Brown in Maryland and Louisiana, Slatter and Somerville concocted a plan so audacious that it would include the involvement of the highest office in the state.[8] Somerville signed a sworn affidavit charging Isaac Brown "with the crime of assault with intent to kill him." The sympathetic Governor Thomas G. Pratt, himself a slave owner, who had recently suffered the indignity of having one of his own slave women escape, acted upon his word.[9]

On April 26, 1847, Governor Pratt issued a requisition to Governor Francis R. Shunk of Pennsylvania, requesting the arrest of Brown on an attempted murder charge and delivery of him to the official Maryland agent, John Zell.[10] According to the United States Constitution, "a person charged in any State, with treason, felony, or other crime, who shall flee from justice, and be found in another State, shall on demand of the

STATE OF MARYLAND—To wit:

Thomas G. Pratt Governor of the State of Maryland,

To His Excellency, the Governor of *Pennsylvania*

IT APPEARS BY THE ANNEXED PAPERS, duly authenticated according to the laws of this State, that *Isaac Brown late of Calvert County stands charged on indictment in Calvert County Court with the crime of an assault upon Alexander Somerville with intent to kill him.*

and it has been represented to me that *he has* fled from the justice of this State, and *has* taken refuge within the State of *Pennsylvania*

Now Therefore, Pursuant to the provisions of the Constitution and Laws of the United States in such case made and provided, I do hereby request that the said *Isaac Brown*

be apprehended and delivered to *John Zell*

who *is* hereby duly authorized to receive and convey *him* to the State of Maryland, there to be dealt with according to law.

In Witness Whereof, I have hereunto affixed my name, and the Great Seal of the State, this *eleventh* day of *May* in the year of our Lord One thousand Eight hundred and *forty seven*

BY THE GOVERNOR:

Thomas G. Pratt

Wm. T. Wootten Secretary of State.

Governor Thomas Pratt of Maryland sent an official request to the governor of Pennsylvania to have Isaac Brown extradited to answer to the charge of "assault with attempt to kill" Alexander Somerville.

Executive authority of the State from which he fled, be delivered up, to be removed to the State having jurisdiction of his crime." Accepting the requisition at face value as he was legally compelled to do, Shunk acted quickly and the next day issued an order to Judge Anson V. Parsons "or any other Judge or Justice of the Peace in this Commonwealth" to issue a warrant to any officer of Philadelphia to apprehend, secure, and deliver Brown to Zell. The governor's order never reached the hands of Judge Parsons, but instead was received by John Swift, the mayor of Philadelphia, who issued the arrest warrant. A few days passed, allowing time for Zell to travel from Baltimore to Philadelphia to meet with local constables and for the legal processes to be put into motion. On Sunday, May 2, armed with a warrant from the mayor, Zell, along with Philadelphia officers William Young and Daniel Bunting, appeared at the Pine Street home and took the stunned Brown into detention and placed him overnight in the northeast police station house on Cherry Street until he could be conveyed to Maryland the next day to — supposedly — stand trial on the charges.[11]

Word of Brown's arrest quickly spread throughout the black community and a large group assembled to express their outrage. They quickly saw through the ruse that Brown was going to be extradited for trial on the charge of attempted murder, knowing that in fact he was only going to be re-enslaved. Communication was made to influential friends who were members of the Pennsylvania Society for Promoting the Abolition of Slavery. They quickly set up an Acting Committee to devote themselves to Brown's case.[12] Before the day was over, a group besieged Judge Parsons, telling him of the injustice, and asked him to intervene. Unaware of the governor's or the mayor's involvement, and thinking the request reasonable, Parsons issued a writ of *habeas corpus,* the official Latin term for the order of a judge to a prison official ordering that an inmate be brought to the court so it can be determined whether or not that person is imprisoned lawfully and whether or not he should be released from custody. *Habeas corpus* is described as the fundamental instrument for safeguarding individual freedom against arbitrary and lawless state action. Parsons directed this writ to John Zell, who was considered to have possession of Isaac Brown, and directed them both to appear before him the next day.

The next morning, on May 3, lawyers, members of the abolition society, female members of the Society of Friends (commonly known as "Quakers") and a large black delegation filled the first floor court room at Congress Hall to witness the official hearing at the Court of Common Pleas with Judge Parsons, along with Senior Judge Edward King presiding.[13] The future proceedings continued to draw large numbers of supporters with the courtroom packed, the outer halls full, and the overflow crowd milling about outside. The building had a special significance to the American people, having been the location of the second inauguration of President George Washington and the home of Congress for the decade when Philadelphia was the capital of the newly formed United States. At that time the Senate met on the upper floor and the House of Representatives on the main floor below.

The courtroom itself was designed to inspire decorum and obedience, with the judges perched behind an elongated desk on an elevated platform, high above those in attendance. The recording clerk sat at a small desk, immediately below the judges. Slightly forward to both the left

Thomas Earle served as legal counsel on several other anti-slavery cases. In 1840, he unsuccessfully attempted to wield more political clout for his causes by running for vice-president of United States in 1840 on the Liberty ticket with James G. Birney.

Courtesy of Friends Historical Library, Swarthmore College, Pennsylvania.

and the right were tables and chairs for the lawyers. Benches for jurors ascended at right angles on either side like small choir lofts in a church. The crowd was separated from the principals by a wooden railing that ran the width of the room. The shackled Isaac Brown stood at centre focus within a waist-high iron-barred prisoner enclosure, dwarfed and intimidated by those who held his future in their hands.

Abolitionist lawyers Thomas Earle, Edward Hopper, Charles Gibbons, and, later, David Paul Brown, stood for the defence — a stance recorded by a fellow lawyer as whose "championship of so desperate and so unpopular a cause demanded physical, no less than moral courage on the part of its advocates. The bar as a body, conservatively gave it the cold shoulder, and Mr. Hopper and his associates were, in truth, the victims, frequently of positively uncivil treatment at the hands of their brother lawyers."[14]

The defence team, who appeared immune to any societal pressures, were particularly imposing. Charles Gibbons, whose father had been an active member of a society founded to protect free blacks from kidnapping and had saved or rescued many slaves from the Baltimore slave markets, was the speaker of the Senate; the soft-spoken but brilliantly articulate Thomas Earle was a former United States vice-presidential candidate for the Liberty Party; Edward Hopper, the son of anti-slavery giant Isaac T. Hopper, who always dressed in the grey conservative Quaker attire, was a witty and amiable personality and had a very large practice; David Paul Brown was renowned for his powers of persuading jurors with his oratorical skills and courtroom theatrics replete with a prominently displayed gold snuff box, elaborate clothing, conspicuous jewellery, and "dandified manners."[15] In this case, the lawyers took aim at the particular issue of the charge that Isaac Brown had "fled from the justice of that State." They were prepared to persuasively argue that this could not possibly be the right man as Brown had never voluntarily fled from Maryland.

Gibbons spoke first, vehemently calling the charge a "gross fraud and an imposition upon the Governor" with the only intention being to return an "alleged" fugitive slave to bondage. Clearly taken by surprise at the scope of the argument and the upper level of government involvement, Judge Parsons told the court that he was not even aware

Library of Congress Prints and Photographs Division. LC-DIG-pga-03855.

This scene, with Independence Hall in the centre and Congress Hall the smaller building to its right, was the location for Isaac Brown's legal hearings in Philadelphia. Published in 1875 by Thomas Hunter.

of Governor Shunk's warrant or he would never have issued the writ of *habeas corpus* and would have simply issued a warrant to deliver Isaac Brown into John Zell's custody. The judge announced that legally he could only address the issue of establishing that Brown was indeed the person named in the warrant.

Zell protested that this was indeed the proper Isaac Brown who had betrayed his own whereabouts in the intercepted letter that he had sent to Calvert County. Ignoring the argument, Gibbons attempted to buy time by telling the judge that an emissary had been sent to the governor to lay the true facts before him rather than the faulty information that he had formerly received. The perplexed judge, not wishing to appear to question the judgement of his superior, expressed that he had to presume that Governor Shunk would not have acted until he was confident that he was fully informed and that the case was strong. Judge King concurred, stating that it was his duty to carry out the views of the governor.

Gibbons would not back down and mentioned several precedents and points of law to back up his argument. Finally, Judges Parsons and King agreed to take a recess to await the response of the governor and to allow time for Zell to produce evidence as to the identity of the accused. Pennsylvania newspapers shared the touching scene of wife Susannah and his children, who had at some time arrived in Philadelphia, weeping outside the courtroom as Isaac Brown was retained in custody without opportunity of bail and placed in the Moyamensing Prison. Across the state line, the *Baltimore Sun* copied the same article verbatim — with the exception of the image of Brown's heartbroken family — in its columns.[16]

When court resumed at 4:00 p.m. the following afternoon, the Maryland delegation was well-prepared. They now had a powerful lawyer, Edward Duffield Ingraham, who, despite being from Pennsylvania, devoted some of his career ruling on returning fugitive slaves from Philadelphia to Southern states.[17] Perhaps his sympathies were influenced by having married a woman from Maryland.[18]

In order to respond to Judge Parsons's demand of the previous day, the Maryland prosecutors had brought in two different men — both slave traders who should know — to positively identify Brown. One was Hope Slatter's agent, Thomas C. Wilson, who had often seen Brown in the Baltimore slave pen in 1845. The other was Samuel Y. Harris, who had purchased Brown from Somerville and then quickly resold him to Slatter. Harris had travelled 185 miles to Philadelphia, supposedly just to confirm the identification. It took little imagination to realize that these men were expecting to be handsomely reimbursed for their travel by being given the reward of being able to resell Isaac Brown yet again.

During the course of cross-examination, Charles Gibbons pointedly asked Wilson what would appear to be the definitive question that would unequivocally settle the case: "Did not Mr. Slatter send Isaac Brown to Louisiana, and was he not sold in that State?" Mr. Ingraham objected to the question and the judge inexplicably agreed and ruled in his favour. The query was left unanswered.

A short testimony by Samuel Y. Harris followed, confirming that he recognized Isaac Brown from having seen him in the Prince Frederick jail where he was held on suspicion of having shot Alexander Somerville.

Evasive and dishonest with the facts, Harris stated that he believed Brown was in jail for only two days "before they took him to Schlatters yard in Baltimore" and he had never seen Brown again until this day. Harris made no mention of having purchased or sold him. Ingraham coolly rested his case asserting that the prisoner's identity had been clearly established and requested that Brown be surrendered to the agent from Maryland.[19]

It was then Charles Gibbons's turn to voice his objections. He passionately claimed to have the right to bring all of the facts of the case into the light. He again stated what everyone in the courtroom already knew — that the case was simply a vicious trick to attempt the legal kidnapping of Brown and that the governor had not been presented with the truth. A hesitant Judge Parsons agreed to let the arguments be made and the case played out.[20] Allowing the animated Gibbons to catch his breath, his impressive and dignified partner, the tall, always elegantly dressed Thomas Earle went on the offensive. Earle continued at length, questioning in lawyer jargon the fine legal philosophy as to whether the governor was acting as an officer of Pennsylvania or of the entire United States, until, to the relief of many in attendance, court was mercifully adjourned for the day.

The legal manoeuvring continued, both in the forefront and behind the scenes. Charles Gibbons dispatched an emissary, William Christopher List, who had been present in the court to the state capital in Harrisburg to speak directly to the governor. Gibbons also sent a letter to inform the governor that he had never seen such a widespread and pervasive feeling of sympathy for anyone accused and confided that Judge Parsons did not seem inclined to question the elected head of state's authority. After quoting points of law, Gibbons beseeched the governor to, at the very least, request that the case be closely examined. Appealing to His Excellency's emotions and humanity, Gibbons closed with the request "to give the prisoner his liberty — joy to his wife & large family and defeat this attempted fraud upon the act of assembly"[21]

Co-counsel Thomas Earle also wrote to the governor, enclosing affidavits that proved that Brown had never fled from Maryland. Earle shared his findings about Somerville's shooting and that, although it was illegal in that state for a black to give testimony against a white person, they were allowed to testify for one of their own race. Although there was no one of any colour who could testify as to Brown's guilt, there were several blacks who were willing to assert that he was innocent of the charges, but none were allowed to speak. Instead, the legal case was abandoned — according to sources, with the knowledge and consent of Governor Pratt.[22] To bolster and humanize the correspondence, Earle included the sworn affidavits of Susannah and Lucinda Brown, which gave their version of the past events. Unable to write, mother and daughter signed their names the only way they knew how — with an X.[23]

Unable to write, mother and daughter signed their names the only way they knew how.

Members of the general public, such as James Mott, the respected Quaker and spouse of the more famous abolitionist and women's rights advocate Lucretia Mott, sent similar appeals.[24] Their collective entreaties had the intended effect, as Governor Shunk sent a request to Judge Parsons to suspend further hearings until he could evaluate the case. To assist in this, the governor sought the advice of Benjamin Champneys, the attorney general for Pennsylvania, in interpreting the 1793 Act of Congress that concerned the apprehension and delivery of fugitive slaves. Only a few days earlier, Champneys had written a long and well-considered opinion advising Governor Shunk to refuse to extradite three other runaways to Maryland. In that case, the request had strictly been that the slaves owed their service and labour to their master and had committed a felony under Maryland law by running away. Shunk and Champneys agreed that what may have been a felony in Maryland was no crime in the free state of Pennsylvania. The apologetic tone of Shunk's letter would have done nothing to assuage his counterpart: "I sincerely regret that a difference should exist between the authorities of the State of Maryland with Pennsylvania, in regard to the construction of our common bond of union, I am constrained, respectfully, to decline issuing warrants for the arrest and delivery of the persons named in your said requisitions."[25]

On the surface, Isaac Brown's case was different, inasmuch as he was charged with being a fugitive from justice cited for assault and battery with intent to kill. But the difference was only superficial, with the ultimate intention of returning the accused to slavery being the same. Pennsylvania's stance related to Brown was intended to be a landmark decision, establishing once and for all the issue of conduct in dealing with requisitions to return fugitives to another state. Champneys travelled the eighty miles from Lancaster, Pennsylvania, to attend the Philadelphia court in person and to voice his own request on behalf of the Commonwealth of Pennsylvania that the case be arrested until he could fully investigate it. The appeal was so granted, and the gut-wrenching case ground to a halt pending the attorney general's ruling.[26]

In a cruel irony of timing, the black population of Philadelphia had chosen that day to publicly celebrate the recent passage of a Pennsylvania anti-kidnapping law by the state legislature with programs

James and Lucretia Mott were activists and leaders in the anti-slavery movement for much of their married lives. Isaac Brown was just one of legions of former slaves whom they assisted. In addition to their work, which included raising a large family, the couple travelled extensively to address the social and spiritual issues that they believed in. Lucretia was almost assuredly the "venerable Quaker lady" described on May 15, 1847, in Rhode Island's Newport Mercury, *who sat with the weeping Susannah Brown and four of her children in a carriage in front of Independence Hall nervously watching the mob that had assembled to protest the arrest of Isaac Brown.*

and demonstrations of thanksgiving at area churches and elsewhere.[27] The law, which was advocated by the anti-slavery society and passed by a general assembly of the Senate and the House of Representatives, stated that it was henceforth a criminal offence to carry away or cause to be carried away anyone, or by fraud or false pretence take any free black for the purpose of being sold. Any participants in such a plan would be sentenced to hard labour and solitary confinement for a period no less than five years or more than twelve years. They would also be fined a minimum of $500 and maximum of $2,000 with the amount split between the Commonwealth of Pennsylvania and the person who

By the time this photograph was taken in 1896, the bright marble exterior of Moyamensing Prison had faded in the half century since Isaac Brown had been imprisoned there. The prison was used from 1835 to 1963. Edgar Allen Poe and Al Capone were among the distinguished inmates.

brought forward the prosecution.[28] For the state's African-American community, who were used to having their rights short-changed, the celebrations were now somewhat tempered as they kept close watch on how — and if — the law would be implemented.

In the interim, Isaac Brown languished in jail, nervously awaiting his fate. As would be expected, despite the grandiose exterior that resembled a gothic-styled medieval castle hewn from polished white granite, conditions in Moyamensing Prison were uncomfortable, with 464 prisoners held within, including fifty-eight blacks. Crimes ranged from serious felonies to misdemeanours such as vagrancy.

A philanthropic group, known as the Philadelphia Society for Alleviating the Miseries of Public Prisons, frequently visited to provide moral and spiritual support as well as to make recommendations to ensure that conditions were acceptable. They filed regular reports to record their observations. In one they noted that three tiers of cells were on either side of the extensive corridors and the entire building was lit and ventilated from the roof. One cell block, presumably where Isaac Brown was housed, was reserved for prisoners who had not yet been sentenced. The nine-by-eleven-feet-wide cells had arched ceilings and were said to be well-furnished with each having running water delivered in pipes. The entire building was heated by a long flue that ran under the floor of the first storey. There was a library with a small selection of books available to prisoners. Although it was recorded that the food was well-prepared and available in sufficient quantities, some inmates complained of the lack of variety. Judging by the recent deaths of four black prisoners, caused by inadequate food and ventilation, the report had its flaws.[29]

During the lull in the proceedings, much of the Philadelphia public diverted their attention to the arrival of the miniature "General" Tom Thumb, who was fresh from a triumphant tour of Europe where he was reported to have met with several of the Crown heads, including Queen Victoria, who showered him with expensive gifts. At least one newspaper reported that his receipts from the tour were the equivalent of $750,000. The wag who wrote the article calculated that amount in silver would weigh twenty-three tons and that it would take fifty-five horses to haul the precious cargo.[30] The sixteen-year-old, fifteen-pound, twenty-seven-inch-tall Tom performed three shows a day at the city museum along with his "pigmy ponies, chariot and elfin coachman and footman" who wore cocked hats and wigs. Tom delighted his audiences with impersonations of Napoleon, a highland chief, Frederick the Great, and ancient Romans and Greeks. The mayor hosted him in his home and the female "beauties" and "elites" flocked around the diminutive charmer. He claimed to have been currently engaged to eight different women, which he modestly claimed to be enough for any one person.[31]

But despite whatever events were happening around the city, focus remained upon the Brown case. The black population of Philadelphia was becoming increasingly agitated. The editor of the *Pennsylvania Freeman* tried to incite its readers into a frenzy of indignation over the trampling of the rights of one of the God's creatures. The principal penny newspapers of Philadelphia, the *Sun* and *Spirit of the Times*, did likewise by publishing details of Brown's brother's brutal death at the hands of Somerville and the lack of any evidence of Brown being the one who had shot Somerville. The newspapers also relayed the injustice of the imprisonment of the innocent daughter Lucinda Brown for several days and her father's forced exile away from his wife and twelve children (contrary to the eleven children recorded elsewhere) when he was sold to Slatter and then to the Deep South. The *Freeman* went even further by publicly challenging Judge Parsons to have the courage to stand up for right "though his decision shall put all Baltimore, aye! all Maryland in a blaze."[32] The flavour of the reports in the Maryland newspapers differed a great deal, informing their readers of the injustices they were being subjected to.[33]

The Maryland contingent, not wanting to delay by awaiting the ruling of Pennsylvania Attorney General Benjamin Champneys, attempted to make pre-emptive measures. A grand jury in Calvert County was hurriedly organized, which formally indicted Isaac Brown. The jurors had apparently already decided Brown's guilt ruling that he:

[W]ith force and arms at the County aforesaid in and upon the said Alexander Somerville in the peace of God and the State of Maryland then and there causing did make an assault with an intent ... then and there feloniously wilfully and of his malice aforethought to Kill and Murder and other wrongs to the said Alexander then and there did to the great Damage of the said Alexander against the act of Assembly in such case made and provided and against the peace government and dignity of the State.

The document continued at considerable length with similar wording so as to leave no doubt of the Grand Jury's stance.[34]

Thomas George Pratt completed his term as governor of Maryland in January 1848. His political retirement was short-term as the General Assembly elected him to the United States Senate. During the Civil War, the Northern forces were suspicious of him because of his pro-slavery views and confined him for several weeks.

Armed with this, on May 11, Governor Pratt again presented a requisition to Pennsylvania's governor with all of the formal requirements of the law addressed. When it arrived the next day, Attorney General Champneys was just finishing writing his opinion, which incidentally found that the earlier requisition was not sufficient to hold Brown in custody. However, in consequence of the secretary of state advising Champneys of the new requisition, his work was outdated and was set aside.[35] Shunk revoked the previous warrant and instructed Judge Parsons that a new one had been issued.[36] Parsons received the letter on Friday, May 21, and prepared for court on Monday morning, at which time he would release Isaac Brown to the agents from Maryland. The next day's edition of the *Public Ledger* informed its readers of the latest development. The attorney general and the governor had reviewed the law and made their ruling. It appeared that all legal avenues were closed and Judge Parson's direction was clear.

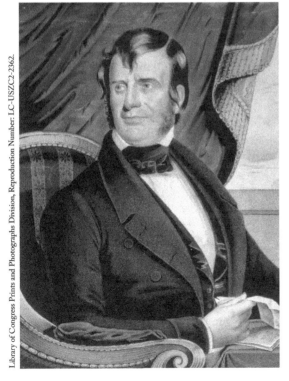

Pennsylvania Governor Francis Rawn Shunk won a second term in office the same year as the Isaac Brown affair. He contracted tuberculosis the next year and was forced to resign. Shunk died on July 20, 1848.

It equally accords with the first principles of free institutions, and the inculcations of our national and State constitutions, that the personal liberty of an individual, and especially where he is about to be removed to another State for trial, should be carefully shielded from commitment, unless by satisfactory evidence upon oath or affirmation, affording probable cause to believe the party to be guilty of the offence with which he is charged. The Affidavit in the present case was made, eighteen months after the alleged offence was committed; in which, the complainant deposes, that he was fired upon and dangerously wounded, on the 23rd October, 1845, and, that he has reason to believe, and does verily believe, that a certain negro man named Isaac Brown was the person who committed the assault. After a careful examination of this affidavit, I consider it as wanting in the expression of that certainty of knowledge as to the commission of the offence, by the prisoner, which renders it insufficient to authorize a warrant for his removal.

Although in England it does not seem to be absolutely necessary, to set out the charge or offence, or evidence, in a warrant to apprehend; yet it is necessary, even there, to set out the charge with distinctness, in the warrant of commitment' and one of the most eminent writers upon Criminal Law (Hale) says, that regularly the warrant out to contain specially the cause of arrest.

The constitutions of all our States wisely protect the personal liberty of the citizen, by prohibiting the issue of any warrant, without probable cause, supported by oath or affirmation.

In the anxiety to secure individuals from unjust accusation, it was at one time held in England, that no person could be deprived of his liberty for any offence, until the finding of a bill against him by a grand jury, which afforded probable and judicial evidence that he was guilty' and all the deviations from this rule, have been considered by some writers as encroachments on the common law. The rule however, long since established there, that the party may be arrested on suspicion before indictment found, became essentially necessary to secure society against the various depredations of crime, by adopting the most efficient measures for the prompt detection and arrest of all persons charged with the commission of offences.

Mr. Champneys's letter to Governor Shunk, May 15, 1847.[37]

Feeling that all was now lost, the news sent a wave of terror, desperation, and heartbreak over Brown and his allies.

Chapter *Five*

Let My People Go

Go down, Moses,
Way down in Egypt's Land
Tell ol' Pharaoh,
Let my people go.

— Traditional

On Monday morning, May 24, the time arrived in the Court of Quarter Sessions for the final disposition of the case. Miles away, the day's edition of the *Baltimore Sun* confidently reported that the Maryland officials had finally tidied up any loose legal threads and had prepared a foolproof offence. Judge Parsons had already been quoted in a Philadelphia newspaper that he would turn Brown over to the Maryland officials "unless some good reason be shown to the contrary."

At 10:00 a.m., Judge Parsons called the court to order and sent a deputy sheriff to the prison to bring Isaac Brown forward. To his surprise, he learned that there was no prisoner to bring! To make matters worse for the judge, he had unwittingly brought the blame upon himself. After receiving the order from the governor to issue a warrant for Brown's arrest, Parsons ignored that technicality because Brown was already secured behind prison bars. Knowing this, the exhausted but vigilant defence lawyers, who worked into the wee hours of Saturday night, had taken advantage of a small window of opportunity to uncover an obscure and long-disused law to have their client released. Well-connected and wise enough to avoid approaching Judge Parsons with the tactic, the defence lawyers instead went to John Bannester Gibson, the chief justice of the Supreme Court of Pennsylvania. After receiving a full explanation and conducting a hasty investigation on precise points of law, Chief Justice Gibson signed a writ *de homine replegiando* to order the sheriff of Philadelphia to release Brown. The writ, simply stated, was to restore to liberty a person who was unlawfully held in custody. In this particular case, the old warrant for Brown's arrest had been revoked and a new warrant had never been issued — consequently he was being illegally held — therefore he was entitled to be released.[1] This was only the second time in Pennsylvania legal history that this writ had been issued, and the first time successfully so.

Late Saturday night, the bar on the door of Brown's cell in Moyamensing Prison was quietly removed. Given the hour, the prisoner had already gone to bed and was in a deep sleep. When Charles Gibbons tried to rouse him, the troubled Brown awoke in a panic, trying to protect himself, believing that he was being seized to be taken back to Maryland. He slowly came to the realization that it was not a fiendish apparition or a

David Paul Brown, one of the defence lawyers in many anti-slavery legal cases, including that of Isaac Brown, was also well known for his literary interests and dramatic flair.

real-life kidnapper, but rather the friendly face of his lawyer. Submitting to the reality that it was neither a waking nightmare nor an impossible dream, he was led to the outer doors and, "to his unspeakable joy," Isaac Brown was set free![2]

A livid, and probably humiliated, Parsons ordered that Anthony Freed, who was the keeper of the prison, be committed to jail himself for allowing the prisoner to make his escape. It was cool comfort that Parsons stated that he "had a high personal regard" for the jail-keeper.[3] In an almost comic twist, Freed had to take himself into custody. Because of his position as the head of the prison, there was no one else authorized to do it. To ensure that Freed did not allow himself any special liberties with his own liberty, bail was set at $1,000. Freed protested that he had released the prisoner under the direction the high sheriff of the county who acted upon a writ that bore the seal of the Supreme Court of Pennsylvania. Neither Freed nor the sheriff nor the sheriff's legal advisor, another Pennsylvania judge, had ever seen this type of writ before and at first declined to follow it. They only complied when Gibbons threatened to sue them for neglect of duty of their office.[4] Upon examination of the order that Freed had been presented with on Saturday night, it is no wonder that he had acquiesced to the order from Judge Gibson:

> The Commonwealth of Pennsylvania to the Sheriff of Philadelphia county, greeting: — We command you that justly and without delay you cause to be released Isaac Brown, whom Anthony Freed, late of your County, took, and taken doth hold, as it is said, unless the aforesaid Isaac Brown was taken by our special precept of our Chief Justice, or for the death of any man, or any other right whereof, according to the laws and usages of this Commonwealth, he is not reprievable, that no more clamor we may have for defect of justice; and how you shall execute this, our writ, you make appear to our justices of our Supreme Court of Pennsylvania, at our Supreme Court, to be holden at Philadelphia, in and for the Eastern District, on the last Monday of July next, and

have you then there this writ. Witness the Honorable John Bannester Gibson, Esquire, Doctor of Laws, Chief Justice of the Supreme Court of Pennsylvania.[5]

Judge Parsons dismissed this argument and defied the power of the Supreme Court of the state, stating that "no court on earth has power to discharge a prisoner committed under a warrant" from his own court. Parsons admonished poor Freed, who had unwittingly placed himself in the legal crossfire, saying that he should have consulted with his court before taking any action.[6]

Parsons was in for another surprise that morning as Brown's lawyers declared that they had now prepared to go on the offensive. Confident in their case and emboldened by their ingenuous defensive tactics that led to the release of their client, they wished to make a further statement that former slaves were not fair game in the state of Pennsylvania. They introduced a civil suit in the District Court on the charge of conspiracy: *Isaac Brown vs. Alexander Somerville, Thomas C. Wilson, Samuel Y. Harris and John Zell.* By then, everyone following the case knew that Brown was not a fugitive from the state of Maryland. Of course, he actually was a fugitive from Louisiana, but that had no relevance to this particular case. The lawyers presented an affidavit dated and signed with an X on May 22, 1847, on behalf of their absent client, which gave Isaac Brown's own account of learning of Somerville's shooting, his arrest and whippings in the Prince Frederick jail, his sale to Slatter and subsequent shipping from Baltimore to the south in a ship that he believed (contrary to the *Victorine's* manifest) carried 169 other slaves, and his resale along with a few other men, to a planter in New Orleans.

Interestingly, he stopped at that point, never revealing the details of his flight and ultimate arrival in Philadelphia other than recording that he had lived in that city "for upwards of one year," leaving that episode open to conjecture — did he stow away on a northbound Mississippi riverboat or in a sail or steamboat that retraced the voyage of the slaver *Victorine*? Did he flee for months across country, first hiding in the Louisiana bayous then travel through slave territory only at night before finding his way to Pennsylvania? Was he helped along the way by a sympathetic crew member of a ship or by humanitarian farmers willing to share a meal or provide an overnight hiding place in a loft? Details on his arrival to Philadelphia; how and when his family was able to join him; why only nine of his eleven children came to Pennsylvania — were all left unsaid, causing those who had embraced his case, both then and in the future, to want to know more.[7]

Charles Gibbons initiated proceedings for the arrest of the four named conspirators, who were to be held in custody pending payment of $5,000 bail. Somerville and his cohorts had spent a great deal of money on their bogus case and suddenly found the tables completely turned against them. The sheriff, who had their arrest warrants, was waiting outside the courtroom, prepared to arrest them the moment they exited the building. Thinking quickly, Ingraham, who had began the day as a prosecuting attorney against Isaac Brown, but had suddenly became lawyer for the defence of Somerville *et al.*, made a motion to Judge Parsons to allow them to leave the court house unmolested because they were only there because they were witnesses in the case against Brown, and, as such, they were entitled to travel to and from the courthouse unmolested. A frazzled and still angry Parsons agreed and granted the motion, warning the sheriff that he would find himself in great difficulty if he attempted to lay a hand on the accused. They prudently used the first public conveyance to return to Maryland.[8]

While all of this was playing itself out, the *Sun* gleefully suggested that Brown would no doubt be safe in Canada.[9] The news spread with "electric rapidity" throughout Philadelphia and the newspapers remarked that the city had never witnessed such jubilation. On May 27, 1847, the appropriately named *Pennsylvania Freeman* trumpeted:

> This is a most glorious result, and one in which we greatly rejoice. We rejoice on account of the poor victim who has escaped a fate terrible to contemplate. Had he been delivered up and taken back to the South, his tortures would have been of the most horrible kind. All that an appetite whetted for vengeance could devise, or the desire of making an example inflict, would have been

visited upon the fugitive by the slave-trader's remorseless underling or the slaveholder's brutal overseer. We rejoice too on account of his wife and large and dependent family of children. What their sufferings would have been when the time of separation had come, can best be imagined by those who witnessed their anguish at the mere probability of such an event. We rejoice too, on account of the vindicated law, and public sentiment of Pennsylvania, and the lesson that has been taught to Southern kidnappers. Pennsylvania is no longer to be a successful or even a safe hunting ground for human bloodhounds. The people have embodied their feelings on this subject in a law, and this law is neither to be set aside or evaded. Neither force nor artifice — let the men-hunters of Maryland and Virginia learn — are hereafter to be of any avail to them in the prosecution in this State of their infamous business. The public sentiment fully sustains the law both in its letter and purpose, and will cause it to be respected.

Conversely, southern newspapers expressed the anger at the result that was felt by many of their readers. The disgust of the editor of the New Orleans *Daily Picayune* — the very same newspaper that had earlier carried runaway slave ads for Isaac Brown — was somewhat typical as he informed the public of the release of Brown and what followed:

> The slave was then hocused off for Canada. Proceedings are to be instituted against the jailor, but no one supposes he will be harmed. The whole case, about which we have not thought it worth while to say much, only shows Southerners that they are not to expect justice even in the Northern States in endeavouring to recover their property.[10]

The tone of the coverage in the north was more similar to that of the *Pennsylvania Freeman* as newspapers from various cities, including Gettysburg, Pennsylvania, Bellows Falls, Vermont, and Washington, D.C., carried the story in detail. Praise was heaped upon the ingenuous defence team — particularly upon Charles Gibbons, who doggedly led the fight and who was credited in uncovering the obscure legal precedent that set Brown free. Thomas Earle was also singled out for being "unwearying in his vigilance and fidelity." Although Edward Hopper and David Paul Brown were less visible in the case, they too were recognized for their background work and readiness to assist.[11] The twelve members present at the June meeting of The Pennsylvania Society for Promoting the Abolition of Slavery unanimously voted to make a donation of $25 each to Charles Gibbons and Thomas Earle "for their Noble and Distinguished Labour in the Defense of I. Brown and by which

Photograph by F. Gutekunst, Philadelphia. Courtesy of Friends Historical Library, Swarthmore College, Pennsylvania.

The Executive Committee of the Pennsylvania Anti-Slavery Society was actively involved in helping Isaac Brown and his family. The members in this photograph, taken about 1851, are: (rear, l–r) Mary Grew, Edward M. Davis, Haworth Wetherfield, Abby Kimber, James Miller McKim (editor of the Pennsylvania Freeman), *and Sara Pugh; seated (l–r): Oliver Johnson, Margaret Jones Burleigh, Benjamin C. Bacon, Robert Purvis, Lucretia Mott, and James Mott.*

Ingenious Means an Innocent Man was snatched from the Pangs of Slavery when almost within its Grasp."[12]

At the behest of Charles Gibbons, members of the Society, including Edward M. Davis, the son-in-law of James and Lucretia Mott, along with a group of six or seven others, published twenty thousand copies of an eight-page pamphlet entitled *Case of the Slave Isaac Brown: An Outrage Exposed* that outlined the history of the case.[13] The antislavery office in the city distributed them at no charge and the Quaker publication *Friends Weekly Intelligencer* also quickly inserted the contents into their May 29 and June 26 editions. On June 15, a large public meeting of the black citizens of the city and county of Philadelphia joined together at Little Wesley Church (which was only a block away from Brown's former home on Pine Street) to praise Senator Charles Gibbons, as well as the *Times* and *Sun* for their "manly and uncompromising editorials in defending his rights, not within the narrow confines of complexional distinction, but upon the broad platform of the rights of man." The group also chimed in the chorus of condemning Parsons and King "having observed with sorrow mingled with indignation the base truckling of our Judges and others in authority to a slaveholding dictation so replete, so palpably manifested in the case of Isaac Brown."[14]

The Philadelphia press also carried articles containing the charge to the Grand Jury in the case of Anthony Freed by a bitter Judge Parsons, who felt he had been portrayed the mean-spirited fool. Parsons complained of the existence of the pamphlet on Isaac Brown that was being "insidiously circulated in the community" and he further deprecated Anthony Freed for his "utter prostitution of all legal processes." Parsons warned the public not to be swayed by anything related to the case of Isaac Brown that had received so much attention because it was related to "one of the exciting topics of the day." His final admonition: "let the law be vindicated and do not let the sympathy for an unfortunate race warp your judgments."[15] Despite Parson's animated charge to the Grand Jury, the twenty-two members, after having considered assessing the judge himself for court costs for initiating this frivolous charge, unanimously voted to ignore it altogether.[16]

Despite all the legal wrangling, editorial proselytizing, moral debating, and differing opinions, everyone — at least publicly — seemed to agree that Isaac Brown was safe from prosecution in the Queen's Dominion of Canada. How wrong they were!

Chapter Six

One More River to Cross

O, Jordan bank was a great old bank,
Dere ain't but one more river to cross.
We have some valiant soldier here,
Dere ain't but one more river to cross
O, Jordan stream will never run dry,
Dere ain't but one more river to cross
Dere's a hill on my leff, and he catch on my right,
Dere ain't but one more river to cross.[1]

— From *Army Life in a Black Regiment*

The Brown home at 172 Pine Street had been completely vacated. Susannah and her children would take no chance that the location of their husband and father could never again be traced through them. The family had already been separated for extended times and they had endured the anguish of the recent legal proceedings. The return of runaway slaves was handled differently in the many jurisdictions in the many northern states and there was no certainty that Isaac Brown would be safe in any of them. The widespread coverage of his story and its final disposition in Pennsylvania invited Alexander Somerville, Hope Slatter, the governor of Maryland, and others to make further attempts to recapture him. Flight to Canada appeared to be the best — perhaps the only — option. But getting a family of two adults and nine children there without attracting undue notice was quite a different matter. Depending upon their route, the journey would be six hundred miles, maybe more. They would have no other option than to take very public means of transportation — trains cross-country and a boat across the Great Lakes. Bounty hunters, doubly inspired by recent events, might be lurking at every station and port along the way to recapture the now famous fugitive. A period of hiding out until the high-profile case began to fade somewhat from the fore of the public consciousness seemed the prudent course of action.

One thing was certain, Pennsylvania was not safe. Luckily, the anti-slavery societies such as the branch in Philadelphia and Underground Railroad operatives that were liberally sprinkled throughout the northern states were well-connected and in regular communication with one another. Two major assemblies had taken place in the month that Isaac Brown had been in custody: the annual meeting of the American Anti-slavery Society that began on May 11 in New York and the New England Anti-Slavery Convention that took place in Boston on May 25. The remarkable and well-publicized proceedings in the Philadelphia case would certainly have been a prominent subject for conversation, particularly in Boston, coming as it did so soon after Brown's release.

Some of the attendees, such as James and Lucretia Mott, would have been especially familiar with the intimate details. The long-standing and exceptionally well-respected Quaker couple were on warm terms with the officers of the convention: president Francis Jackson and secretary Edmund Quincy, both of whom also held those same positions with the board of managers of the Massachusetts Anti-Slavery Society. William Lloyd Garrison, the most prominent national abolitionist leader, who served as president of the American Anti-slavery Society and editor of the most influential anti-slavery newspaper, the *Liberator*, was also in attendance, as was Frederick Douglass, the most prominent black leader of the era.[2] An unnamed "fugitive slave from Louisiana" in the audience was also introduced to address the crowd. At first he could not find the words to speak, but after giving way on the podium to another fugitive who spoke of his escape, he became emboldened enough to tell the crowd that he "wished the hall was five million times bigger than it was and that his voice was like six million thunders to fill it."[3]

This African-American Church in Boston is identified as the Twelfth Baptist Church with its congregation dating from 1840. Leonard A. Grimes, who became pastor there in 1848, was active in the Underground Railroad. In 1887, William J. Simmons, author of Men of Mark: Eminent, Progressive and Rising, *wrote on page 664: "hundred of escaping slaves passed through his hand en route to Canada." Several other notable black figures, including Lewis and Harriet Hayden, Shadrach Minkins, Anthony Burns, and Thomas Sims, were members.*

Although the identity of this fugitive from Louisiana is uncertain and other details are of necessity shrouded in secrecy, it is clear that Isaac Brown — who once again became "Samuel Russell" — along with his family, was quietly whisked away to New York City, which had its own sophisticated anti-slavery community.[4] It was there that he met with executive members of the American Missionary Association.[5] Arrangements were made that the Brown family was to be taken under the wing of Reverend Samuel Young, a forty-one-year-old Congregationalist minister from nearby Williamsburg, Long Island, who was also a friend of the Hopper family, who were so personally involved in the Brown case.

A view of Boston near the time that the Browns arrived there. Published by N. Currier, circa *1848.*

Francis Jackson was one of the most prominent anti-slavery activists and beloved among his peers. More than just a moral theorist, he is credited with welcoming many runaways into his home.

Reverend Young had an interesting and occasionally melancholy history of his own. Born in New Jersey to a poor family, he was abandoned and sent out into the world as an orphan. He could never recall having seen his parents' faces or heard their voices. Surviving the many trials of his youth, he came to embrace Christianity and became a dedicated minister. He was never able to overcome poverty in his lifetime, but had no desire to do so. Married with eight children of his own, Young was uniquely capable of empathizing with the individual members of the Brown family.[6]

For over a month, from late May until mid-July, the Browns were hidden away in New York, then in Boston, where they fell under the protection of Francis Jackson, Edmund Quincy, and William Lloyd Garrison. It was not until then that those involved acquired a wavering confidence that it was safe for the family to attempt the trip to Canada, long a favoured destination for fugitive slaves. The Dawn Settlement, near the village of Dresden in southwestern Canada West (now Ontario), was a particularly desirable location and the Boston abolitionists had been generous with their financial support. Two of the founders of Dawn, Hiram Wilson and Josiah Henson, had been in Boston within the month and both had enthusiastically touted the success of the settlement.[7] With this fresh on everyone's mind, it was decided that this would be an ideal destination for the fleeing family. Josiah Quincy Jr., the mayor of Boston, and brother of Edmund Quincy, was able to secure a railroad pass from Boston to Albany, New York, for the Brown family. As an additional safety precaution, the Browns were accompanied by Reverend Young, whose professional demeanour and white skin allowed him more clout in spear-heading the trip.[8]

It was a relief to have an uneventful experience on the more than seven-hour trip to Albany. The landscape that rushed by the train's window would have offered endless fascination for the Brown children. Rolling hills transformed into small mountains, all subtly coloured the entire spectrum of shades of grey. Inexplicably defying the dictates of nature, giant irregularly shaped evergreens competed with hardwood trees for toeholds in the rock fissures. Clusters of white-barked birch trees were occasionally sprinkled into the mix. The new freight house at the Greenbush Station opposite Albany and at the end of the route was a man-made marvel. With walls nineteen feet high and nine feet thick, the building covered two-and-a-half acres and was said to have cost $100,000 to build and was considered to be the largest building in the United States.[9]

It was with this backdrop that they encountered their first snag, which delayed their progress for a full day. The cumulative fare for the next segment of the journey, at $3 per person or four cents per mile, was costly for the group of twelve, and Reverend Young tried to appeal to the person in charge, a Mr. Goming, to have compassion for the Brown family. It was not unknown for the railroad companies to be flexible, in fact, in the same month they had waved the fee for a carload of students from The New York Institution for the Deaf and Dumb travelling home from Albany to Buffalo to visit family and friends. Steamboat captains on the Hudson River made a like offer and the proprietors of the eatery in the Albany Rail Road House refused to accept payment for the students' meals.[10] However, Mr. Goming refused to give free passes on the grounds that the company he worked for was opposed to issuing them to blacks. Reverend Young pleaded their case and implored Goming to reconsider. After considerable begging, Goming relented — in part. He finally agreed to give them free passes from Schenectady to Syracuse, leaving Young and the Browns to solve the dilemma of getting from Albany to Schenectady.[11]

It was an "unpleasant task," but Reverend Young eventually succeeded — perhaps with a competing railroad company — in getting a set of passes for the relatively short eighteen-mile trip from Albany to Schenectady. The trains on this route were immensely popular, sometime carrying between 450 and five hundred passengers crowded into nine of the eight-wheeled passenger cars on a single trip.[12] The group wedged themselves in until they reached Schenectady, where they boarded yet another train for the one-hundred-mile-plus trip to Syracuse, arriving at midnight on Saturday, July 17. They were forced to remain in that city for two days. There would have been a certain comfort for Isaac Brown and his family there. Syracuse was a noted Underground Railroad safe haven with leaders like Jermain Loguen, Reverend Luther Lee, Samuel May, and John Wilkinson.

Lee worked as a lecturer for the New York State Anti-Slavery Society in 1839 and 1840 before becoming a Wesleyan minister, and, in 1843, led his congregation to break away from the Methodist Episcopal Church because the latter refused to speak out against slavery and allowed slave owners to be a part of their congregation. They constructed their own church, which today remains the oldest building in Syracuse. Lee was also an executive member of the American and Foreign Anti-Slavery Society along with Lewis Tappan, William Whiting, Charles B. Ray, and George Whipple, most of whom had some connection with the flight of Isaac Brown.[13]

Reverend Lee would have been able to share some stories of his Underground Railroad activities that would have resonated with Isaac Brown. One in particular would be of a fugitive who was enslaved on a plantation where Henry F. Slatter had taken fifty blacks on speculation.

Lee was well-connected with officials from the railroad company in Syracuse. Because of that, he was always able to secure free passage for any runaways who passed through the city simply by writing "Pass this poor colored man" or "poor colored woman," or in a case like Isaac Brown's, "poor colored family."[14] Lee claimed that all of the conductors understood the pass and never challenged it. Their orders would have come from their superiors including John Wilkinson, a lawyer and president of the Syracuse and Utica Railroad.[15]

Wilkinson's anti-slavery sentiments evolved over time. Seventeen years previously, he had been a vocal attendee at an anti-abolition meeting, at which he chaired a committee to protest those "obnoxious" advocates of immediate emancipation who:

> [H]ave caused great excitement and alarm in the States where Slavery exists, and tend to endanger not only the welfare and happiness of the white population in those States, and the well being of the Slaves themselves; but threaten the subversion of the Union under which this country has for more than half a century enjoyed a state of prosperity and happiness unparalleled in the annals of history.[16]

Referring to Abolitionists as "misguided" and "fanatics and incendiaries of a dangerous order," Wilkinson condemned the formation of abolition societies and the publication of emancipation newspapers and pamphlets.[17] Mercifully, his stance had softened throughout the years or else the recent publication of the pamphlet *The Case of Isaac Brown* and the attendant media coverage would have surely enraged Wilkinson enough to turn Isaac Brown over to the slave hunters. In coming years Wilkinson would speak out, advocating the prohibition of slavery in all United States territories and against allowing any law that would force the apprehension and surrender of fugitive slaves without allowing them due process.[18] He would also grant permission for a mass meeting of an estimated 1,500 people to assemble in the magnificent new domed engine house of the Syracuse and Utica Railroad Company to celebrate the anniversary of the famous "Jerry Rescue" in which a large crowd fought off federal marshals and local police officers to rescue a fugitive slave who had been arrested and threatened to be returned to the South.[19]

With his recently matured sympathy for runaways, Wilkinson was easily persuaded to provide a free pass for the Brown party to take a train from Syracuse to Buffalo. At midnight Monday, after a two-day pause to refresh themselves, the group boarded the train heading west on a rough route that was long and crooked with steep inclines. The plan was that when the cars stopped along the route at Rochester, Brown and Young were to meet with another man who would have confirmed the validity of their pass. However, Young misunderstood the directions he had received from Wilkinson and failed to meet the person. He had yet to grasp the fact that New York State had a huge patchwork of unaffiliated railroad companies with different officials running each one. As a result, the conductor from the Attica and Buffalo Rail Road made an insolent and heated public refusal to let them proceed on their stretch of track without paying. Skilled in the arts of dealing with that type of behaviour, Young produced the pass, which was signed by Wilkinson that read "to Buffalo" and responded to the irate conductor in a manner intended to cause embarrassment to the hard-hearted railroad employee, who stood his ground.[20]

Disappointments and challenges were becoming increasing burdens for the travellers. But Providence intervened to lighten the load in the form of a man who took a keen interest in the beleaguered group. Upon having his sympathy aroused by Isaac Brown's heart-wrenching story, the gentleman, a stove-maker by trade, wrote out a pledge to send a heavy, good-quality stove to the Browns once they had reached Canada. The gift from this stranger would be worth between eighteen and thirty dollars, an amount that the intended recipients could never have afforded.[21]

With their spirits buoyed by this random act of kindness, Reverend Young purchased tickets and the entourage continued their trip to Buffalo on Wednesday July 21, where they were met with another pleasant surprise. The conductor, with whom he had earlier quarrelled, met them at the station, and, in the presence of a lawyer, apologetically refunded the money for their fare. This welcome and unexpected turn of events with the promises of Canada almost within their grasp should have been the ultimate gratifying gesture as the Browns were soon to leave the worries of the United States behind. But Susannah had taken ill, worn out from everything they had experienced. Unable to continue immediately, they were forced to spend another two days in Buffalo.

The timing was unfortunate as there had been a major racial incident near the city only five days previously. An Alabama couple, accompanied by their female slave, were on an excursion to see one of nature's masterpieces, Niagara Falls, and were about to depart when, according to one report, between twenty and thirty blacks rushed the train in an attempt to liberate the girl. Some threw obstructions on the railroad tracks while others rushed the passenger car. The engineers and conductors rushed to assist the slave-owner and violence erupted. Other reports said that a black man was attacked after simply asking the slave girl if she voluntarily wished to go back with her master. Other blacks joined in to defend their fellow. An Alabama newspaper reported that the girl did not want to leave her mistress, while a Washington newspaper reported that the girl had told a hotel chambermaid that her mistress treated her badly and asked that the coloured citizens assist her in escaping. Whatever the facts were, all agreed that the rescue was unsuccessful and several people were seriously wounded. In a general retaliation later that day, a mob fired gunshots and burned down a house that was occupied by blacks.[22]

Perhaps it was the resulting tension that influenced Reverend Young and the Browns to seek a boat headed southwest to cross Lake Erie rather than take one of the nearby ferries that crossed the Niagara River. With Susannah regaining her strength, Young proceeded to plan the final leg of the journey, and boarded a Great Lakes boat, the *St. Louis*, and asked the clerk if he could book passage. The clerk said if it were up to him he would not take blacks, explaining that he had done it once and the man turned out to be a slave. The Southern press learned of it and printed the story to the detriment of the ship's business. When the vessel's master, Captain Wheeler, arrived, he contradicted his clerk, stating: "I will take them. I had as soon take knot heads as pig iron." At first pretending not to show any offence, Young waited until a group of curious onlookers gathered closer, and, using the psychological technique that he had recently honed on a train's conductor, softly asked: "Captain, what kind of a civilization is that which teaches you to speak in such disrespectful term of your fellow-beings?"

The embarrassed captain dropped his head and said that he would take them across the lake. A man of unflagging principle, Reverend Young declined, stating: "I have the honour of travelling with a select family, and if you are a fair representative of the character of the company and crew of this boat, I shall not go."[23] At that, he took his valise and returned to shore, while two crew members tried to persuade him that they would be well treated. Young replied to the well-intentioned men that he would not cross Lake Erie until he could find a civilized captain. It was not until the next day before Young found his man — Captain Croton Shepherd of Ashtabula, Ohio, who commanded the steamboat *Cleveland*. To his delight, Shepherd had heard of Young's dressing down of Captain Wheeler the previous day, and in repayment for that pleasure Shepherd would gladly take the entire Brown family at no cost. Young would have to pay his own fare, but the Captain promised him that he could join him in his state room at any time without charge.

It was an enjoyable forty-eight-hour trip across Lake Erie with Captain Shepherd and his crew before they entered the mouth of the

Detroit River, passed by the old British Fort Malden in Amherstburg to their right, and the island covered with birch and beech trees that the early French settlers had called Bois Blanc to their left, and finally pulled into the dock in Detroit, Michigan. Only minutes and the narrow Detroit River separated them from the Canadian shore at Windsor. However, it took three long days before they could find a boat that intended to travel up the river to Lake St. Clair, their intended destination within the British colony.

While waiting, the Browns and Reverend Young were joined by Hiram Wilson, the missionary to the blacks in Canada, who had prepared a house for the family next to his own in the Dawn Settlement. He had made the sixty-mile trip to Detroit to guide them the rest of the way. Forty-four-year-old Wilson had a long history of selfless service to fugitives. After graduating from the Oberlin Theological Seminary in 1836, he travelled to what was then Upper Canada to observe the progress of blacks there. Returning the next year as a representative of the American Anti-Slavery Society, he began a quest to raise money and establish mission schools throughout the province. By 1839, he had established ten schools with fourteen teachers who instructed three hundred students. With the zeal and dedication of an Old Testament prophet, he travelled thousands of miles, criss-crossing the land separating the Great Lakes. Many of his journeys were on foot, covering fifty miles per day. He carried a valise containing a bit of food and he took shelter for the night in whatever household would offer it. Generous beyond reproach, he and his family lived a life of poverty and want.[24]

Wilson had been in Boston when Isaac Brown had first been arrested in Philadelphia, attempting to raise money for the mission dubbed "The British American Institute" that he had helped to found as part of the Dawn Settlement. He had sympathy for the man, as he did for everyone who had suffered the curse of slavery. But Wilson was now the recipient of the profound sympathy of others. Earlier that summer, his beloved wife Hannah had died at the Dawn Settlement. During her final illness, her friends asked if they should not immediately send for her husband who was in Boston, many miles away. She refused, knowing that "he was engaged at his post, pleading the cause of the poor and despised descendants of Africa" and that for the sake of doing good she would sacrifice his company.[25] She had been the one constant in his life: his partner in seeing to the needs of the fugitives who came to their door, a teacher at the mission school, and the devoted mother of four small children. It was not until he had arrived in Detroit on his way back from Boston in late May of that year that he learned of her death. With a heavy heart, he hurried home, arriving eight days after her funeral.[26] Taking but a little time to indulge in his own grief, he soon returned to his calling. Within weeks after having received a letter from Francis Jackson in Boston alerting Wilson about the Browns' flight, he returned to Detroit to meet them, now safely in the care of Wilson's anti-slavery friends.

Among those friends was a celebrated lawyer and member of The Michigan State Antislavery Society, Charles H. Stewart. Both he and Hiram Wilson were among the founders of the organization. Stewart had recently run for a seat in Congress on the Liberty ticket, the same party that others, who had helped Isaac Brown, had been associated with.[27] Five years earlier, in a move that had elevated his status among abolitionists on both sides of the border, Stewart had spoken out in protest against the British authorities extraditing Nelson Hackett, a fugitive slave who had been captured in Canada West. When vocal objections failed, Stewart secured a writ of *habeas corpus* for the runaway, when the latter was transferred from Canada to a Detroit jail cell. The official charge against Hackett was that, in making his escape, he had taken his master's gold watch and a beaver coat, as well as a horse and saddle. Although Hackett pled guilty to those charges (a confession that he later recanted, claiming that he had been beaten in the head with the butt of a whip and a large stick during his interrogation), it was felt that, as it was in the case of Isaac Brown, this was only a pretext for having the slave returned to bondage. Hackett was returned in shackles to his master in Arkansas, despite all efforts of Stewart and many others on his behalf.[28] According to one of his fellow slaves, upon Hackett's return to his plantation, he was kept in chains and fetters, flogged unmercifully on several different occasions with the number of lashes ranging from thirty-nine to 150, and finally dispensed to the interior of Texas.[29] Stewart and Wilson had grave concerns that history could repeat itself.

Perhaps Canada was not the safe haven that everyone had assured Isaac Brown it would be. The worries, which were constant companions, increased. And he would still have to eventually cross the Detroit River to the Canadian side to catch a boat bound for the Dawn Settlement. To take that first step, he would have to take the ferry operated by a known slave hunter named Lewis Davenport, who had returned the chained Nelson Hackett part of the way back to Arkansas. Davenport's hard-hearted reputation was further established when he was awarded the contract to build the scaffold and gallows for the last public hanging in Detroit.[30] Terrifying him further were the slave hunters who had been regularly patrolling the Detroit docks for more than a week, looking for runaways.[31]

Chapter Seven

The Sun Came Like Gold
Through the Trees

*When I found I had crossed that line I looked at my hands
to see if I was the same person. There was such a glory over
everything; the sun came like gold through the trees, and
over the fields, and I felt like I was in Heaven.*[1]

— Harriet Tubman

Nine o'clock, Sunday morning, July 25, 1847. It was nearly two years
since Isaac Brown had been arrested and tortured for being suspected of shooting his master. It was more than two full months since
he had crept out of Moyamensing Prison in the middle of the night. The
trip from Boston had taken almost two weeks while others had made
the same trip in half that time. Today he could be breathing the air of
British North America, hopefully free at last and in the company of his
wife and his children.

It had rained incessantly for the past several days and it continued
with a heavy downpour that morning. Although it added to his discomfort, perhaps the weather would diminish the vigilance of the slave hunters as well as ferry-boat owner Davenport. This morning Isaac — still
Samuel Russell for a little while longer — travelled alone to the foot of
Griswold Street, hoping to throw off any observer who might be looking
for a black couple with a large group of children. They could come later,
under the watchful eye of the Reverends Young and Wilson, who had
been preoccupied in solemn conversations with Charles Stewart. The
ploy worked and the trip on the steam-powered ferry *United*, described

The ship in the middle right of the picture entitled "City of Detroit, Michigan. Taken from the Canada shore near the ferry (1837)" has been identified by R. Alan Douglass in Uppermost Canada: The Western District and the Detroit Frontier, 1800–1850 *as Lewis Davenport's ferry, the* United, *the same ferry that Isaac Brown rode to Canada.*

on a sunnier day as "a pretty little steamer, gaily painted, with streamers flying, and shaded by an awning," was uneventful.[2] Sheltering himself against the rain, Isaac climbed the banks on the Windsor side.

Within two days, Isaac was joined by the rest of his family; Reverend Young had long since been included in that kindred designation. The skies finally cleared at the beginning of the week and temperatures turned cool and pleasant. Arrangements were confirmed to take passage on a boat that would take them the final sixty miles across Lake St. Clair, which would then take them into the mouth of the Sydenham, the river that wove its way to the Dawn Settlement situated at its head of navigation. The scenery along the way was pleasing, and something about the passing landscape and the sounds he was leaving behind would have been vaguely familiar to Isaac — the long and narrow layout of the farms measured in arpents rather than the imperial acres, the activity at the wharves with the different races busy working, and, for him, the indecipherable language of the French and the Native people. But now these sights and sounds had a far different feel than the Mississippi had when he first entered the harbour of New Orleans.

The jubilation upon arriving at their destination was somewhat tempered. The entire Brown family were sick. Samuel Young judged that it was a minor malady thinking "it is merely the change of water."[3] Hiram Wilson, surveying the larger picture, saw past the illnesses when writing to George Whipple from the American Missionary Association in New York, asking him to inform those who had a hand in the escape of the outcome: "You will rejoice to learn that Isaac Brown (alias Sam'l Russell) with his numerous & interesting family of a wife & 9 children from the house of bondage reached Dawn on the 28th ult. in good health and spirits."[4]

The Browns would have been impressed upon first inspecting their new home. There were three hundred acres on the British American Institute grounds, which straddled both sides of the winding Sydenham. Nearly one hundred acres of the fertile lands were already cleared and under cultivation. The crops of Indian corn, potatoes, and rye looked good, despite a recent frost that had iced over their leaves. Black walnut trees that only grew naturally on rich soils were abundant, and a steam sawmill was being erected so the timber could be cut and sold to bring revenue to the institute. Plans had been made for the steam engine to also power a gristmill to make flour. The project was under the supervision of a black man formerly from South Carolina, who had acquired the skills of a millwright and designer. Two other men, who were seasoned blacksmiths, were making the boilers, engines, furnaces, and a brick building to house them. The bricks were made on the institute land. A pot-ashery had been started to make use of the ashes from the hardwood trees. Ashes were placed in a large vat and water poured over the top, producing a liquid ash that dripped out the bottom. The solution was then boiled until only a residue, called "black salts" was left. These salts were then fired at a high temperature in the "pot-ashery," creating "pearl ash" that could be used to produce soap, glass, ceramics, and other items.

There was an atmosphere of opportunity and new beginnings in the settlement as befitted the name — Dawn Settlement. A large schoolhouse had been erected, the perfect thing for the many Brown

Courtesy of Buxton National Historic Site & Museum.

Reverend Josiah Henson, pictured here with his wife Nancy, was a co-founder of Dawn Settlement along with Reverend Hiram Wilson. Henson was also close with Boston's abolitionist community, who assisted in the escape of Isaac Brown, and was in Boston at the time of Brown's flight there from Philadelphia. The image appears in Progression of the Race in the United States and Canada *by Rev. D.D. Buck.*

children. With about eighty other students attending, there would be playmates for all. Several modest houses had been built, and, with the exception of one, were occupied. A frame barn was in view. There was a two-storey, twenty-two by thirty-four-foot home constructed of hewn lumber. Another two-storey brick building, thirty-by-thirty-two feet, was even more imposing. Two men, one from North Carolina, the other from Virginia, had built a rope walk across a waterway with cord made from hemp that they had grown.[5]

The press in North America and in Europe had frequently brought the story to the attention of their readers. Hiram Wilson and Josiah

Henson, another of the co-founders of the institute, had travelled extensively on fundraising missions to New England, to the American upper Midwest, and to the British Isles. They were spreading the word and seeking financial support to provide for the basic needs of the penniless fugitives and build the infrastructure for the settlement, which was to include a manual labour school. The philosophy was to promote a practical education that would instill independence and self respect — not the easiest task for a people who had been beaten down and degraded for generations. But Wilson, who would often wax poetical on their progress, regularly witnessed "their joy unspeakable in their inalienable birthright boon to freedom under the mild and benign sway of Victoria's sceptre."[6] In an almost amusing counter to this view, the Maryland *Sun* opined in response to Wilson: "The remarkable point about all this is that the negroes who were always enjoying practical community or Fourierism [a Utopian community] of South, and in a mild climate, should fly to Canada to try Fourierism there."[7]

Isaac and Susannah had much to think about as they surveyed the gently rising landscape, pondering the future and reflecting on the past. The support they had received was almost unbelievable, so much more than others who had been in their place had received. Surrounding them were former slaves who were missing an eye or a hand or a leg. Others had broken noses and missing teeth. Like cattle, some bore the charred design of their master's brand. As a result of being chased while trying to flee, some still had buckshot and rifle balls buried in parts of their bodies. Upon arrival in Canada, some had to cut down a tree and hollow it out to prepare a place to sleep in the winter's cold, surviving on meals of beans or a potato given them by others. One elderly couple claimed to have survived for two days with only grass for nourishment.[8] Indeed, the Browns had much to be thankful for, and Reverend Samuel Young was particularly deserving of their gratitude.

The original plan upon leaving Boston had been that Young would only accompany the family as far as the border. In the letter that Francis Jackson had written to Hiram Wilson to inform him of the case and to ask his friend to meet Isaac Brown in Detroit, Jackson had expressed his high praise, "In his flight he has been accompanied by a most devoted and benevolent white friend, Samuel Young of Williamsburg, N.Y., who will probably see them to the Canada line; there is not a man in ten thousand who would have put himself to so much anxiety, trouble and risk, without a thought of remuneration! Heaven reward him here and hereafter!"[9]

Hiram Wilson was also quickly and thoroughly impressed with Young's character and commitment. In his letter to the American Missionary Association that announced the safe arrival of "Sam'l Russell," Wilson showered praise upon Young and implored the philanthropic organization to do what they could to support his remaining as a permanent missionary in Canada. Many of the black refugees were deeply touched after meeting him and listening to him preach, and were eager for him to stay among them. Young had the same effect on a nearby congregation when he spoke at Sabbath services of the First Nations Mission at Moraviantown.[10]

Reverend Young looked forward to accommodating them. Ever humble and pious, he believed that his sacrifices were but little and that the blessings descended upon him. In a letter to Francis Jackson, he gave thanks for the special treatment he and the Browns had received at his home and expressed his appreciation to everyone who had treated them with such kindness. He promised to stop in Boston on his way back to New York to deliver his thanks in person. Writing from the comfort of the Wilson home, he shared the scene that all had envisioned: "Samuel and his family have a house to themselves a few rods distant."[11]

As the Browns attempted to recuperate from their harrowing experience and settle into their new world, the story of Nelson Hackett's capture and return to the United States hovered over them. Reverend Young, based on the advice of Charles H. Stewart, had already made the decision to delay returning to his family in New York to await a decision as to whether he was going to receive funding to support his proposed missionary endeavours, and to go to the highest official in the Canadas. Once there, he planned to lay the true facts of the Isaac Brown case before him, in the hope of thwarting rumoured efforts by Maryland's Governor Pratt to demand that the fugitive slave be returned.

Chapter Eight

Rescue the Slave

Freemen arouse ye, before 'tis too late,
Slavery is knocking at every gate:
Make good the promise your early days gave,
Christian men, Christian men, rescue the slave.[1]

— From the *Provincial Freeman*

After two days' rest, Samuel Young departed Dawn for the seat of government for British North America's provinces, Canada West and Canada East, in Montreal, presided over by Governor General James Bruce, who bore the aristocratic titles 8th Earl of Elgin and 12th Earl of Kincardine, but was more simply known as Lord Elgin. Young carried copies of the detailed pamphlet of the case that had been printed in Philadelphia, as well as some letters of introduction that had been provided by Isaac T. Hopper, Charles H. Stewart, and Hiram Wilson, which he could present to eminent figures in London, Hamilton, Toronto, Kingston, and Montreal. These figures were selected as those whose names would carry weight with the governor general. It was decided that Samuel Russell/Isaac Brown would not make the trip, fearing that if things did not unfold as hoped, he could be arrested by an official who might easily be deceived if he was unaware of all of the facts. Experience had taught them a valuable lesson.

Hiram Wilson transported Young sixty-five miles by horse-drawn carriage to London, where they parted, promising to meet upon Young's return and to tour other black settlements in Canada West. Young had a warm reception in Toronto, where he met with the influential Colonel John Prince, who had the prestigious position as Queen's Counsel and was a long-time elected member of the House of Assembly. Prince had been partly responsible for the return of Nelson Hackett to the United States and was generally intolerant of blacks, so it was now critical to have him on Isaac Brown's side. It was ironic that Charles Stewart, who had once opposed Prince in the Hackett case, now provided Young with the letter of introduction to his former foe. In this case, Prince gave his support to Brown and encouraged Young to proceed to Montreal.

Young was cordially received there by all of the government officials, with the exception of a chilly silence from Attorney General Henry Sherwood from Canada West, who offered no assistance.[2] Undeterred, Young was well received by Major Campbell, the private secretary of Lord Elgin, and by Attorney General William Badgley of Canada East (now Quebec). Badgley, being from the Francophone province and having regularly witnessed the disharmony between two cultures, perhaps had more empathy for Brown, and thoroughly investigated the terms of the Webster-Ashburton Treaty that addressed the legal issue of extradition between Britain and the United States. After studying the law and the legal documents that Young provided, Badgley gave his assurance that Isaac Brown "was as safe as he would be in London, England" and would not be surrendered to Maryland officials.

The timing was fortuitous. Within two days, two emissaries of the governor of Maryland appeared in Montreal and were granted an audience with Lord Elgin. They demanded the surrender of Brown, but were rebuffed. A defiant Reverend Young met the dejected men as they left the office of the governor general and told them of his part in accompanying the fugitive slave to Canada. "At this announcement they were as fierce and ravenous as wild beasts, and said they would soon lynch him if they had him in Baltimore." Young set aside his usual calm demeanour and invited them to display their bravery on the spot, but the southerners discerned a rising tide of indignation among a gathering crowd of Canadians and decided that discretion was indeed the better part of valour. Still seething, they snarled that they would no longer speak to anyone "who sympathized with niggers" and went on their way, all the while followed by a group who ensured that they would not turn around.[3] An abolitionist acquaintance of Young, who stayed at the same hotel as these two, remarked that prior to their trip to the Government House they were quiet and peaceable, but later "were like mad-men" because Young had thwarted their purpose. They claimed that the governor of Maryland had promised them a reward of $1,000 if they returned with Brown.[4]

Samuel Young prepared to leave the city in triumph. The city was beautiful with its Old World charm, but Young was eager to share the news of his success, see other black settlements, and finally return to his own family where he could make a final decision on moving to Canada. Before departing, he took notice of an overwhelmingly vindictive epidemic that was attacking Montreal. An outbreak of typhus or "ship fever," as it was sometimes called, was spreading throughout the desperate masses of immigrants to Canada who had fled the potato famine in Ireland. It was highly contagious and quickly spread in every filthy and

Of the one hundred thousand Irish immigrants who sailed in overcrowded "coffin ships" across the Atlantic to Quebec in 1847, it is estimated that one in five died. The image is from Frank Leslie's Illustrated Newspaper, *January 12, 1856.*

crammed hold of a ship that left the British ports carrying those "peasants" who were already suffering the effects of famine and exhaustion. Many of those, who witnessed the many burials at sea and survived the voyage in what came to be known as "coffin ships," carried the disease into the crowded harbour at Montreal, unleashing it on the rest of the city. Within about twelve days of exposure, the affected began to suffer with fever, headaches, muscle aches, and weakness, followed by rashes on the torso and limbs. After suffering for up to ten days, as many as six thousand people succumbed to the disease. Montreal was not the place to tarry in the summer of 1847, but Reverend Young, being the person that he was, spent some time giving comfort to the afflicted before taking his leave to stay on schedule to keep promises made to friends.

After rejoining Hiram Wilson as previously agreed, the Long Island minister was able to relay the story of Isaac Brown to a large group in Toronto, who revelled in his account of his reception and success in Montreal. Forty-six Toronto black residents were inspired to make public their appreciation by composing a letter and having it printed in *The Globe*. Part of their motivation was less lofty, as they also attempted to shame Sherwood, the attorney general from their own province, whose duty it was to address the case, for his lack of interest or support.

To the Honourable Wm. Badgley, Attorney
General of Canada East, &c., &c.

We, the undersigned, coloured citizens of
Toronto and vicinity, loyal and dutiful
subjects of her Majesty's just and powerful
government, take pleasure in availing
ourselves of this opportunity to express to
you our sincere thanks for the courteous and
Christian-like manner in which you recently
received our late kind and worthy friend,
the Rev. Samuel Young, of New York, who is
known to have been deeply interested for

the protection and welfare of our afflicted
brethren in the United States of America,
especially as evinced in the case of the
innocent and grossly injured and persecuted
man, who has lately found his way to this
asylum, from the midst of the republican
despotism and slavery.

Forasmuch as we deeply sympathised with our
honoured advocate and brother, above mentioned,
in his philanthropic and praiseworthy
exertions for the deliverance of the innocent
unoffending fugitive from the bloody grasp
of the avaricious man-thief, we cannot
find language adequate to express fully our
grateful obligations to you for giving him the
hand of friendship, and in his worthy course,
such candid and earnest assistance as could
be looked for, only in an official gentleman
possessed of a noble and philanthropic mind.

May the Divine blessing attend you in all
the relations you sustain, even to the end of
your earthly pilgrimage — and especially in
the discharge of the duties which devolve upon
you in your official capacity.

(Signed)W. R. ABBOTT, and forty-five others

Letter from the Coloured Citizens of Toronto to Attorney General Badgley.
The Globe, *December 11, 1847.* [5]

Energized from two days filled with accolades and warmth in Toronto, Young and Wilson boarded a steamboat at the Lake Ontario harbour and proceeded to Hamilton, reaching port at sundown on August 24. Reverend Young's recent fame had already spread to that city and he was met by a messenger, who requested that he come and address a crowd eager to hear first-hand details of the Isaac Brown saga. He did not disappoint, and kept the audience spellbound until late in the night.

The next morning, the two ministers climbed into a stagecoach bound for Waterloo, a trip of forty miles. Their destination was a gateway to the old and established scattered black settlements within the area known as Queen's Bush. After a night's sleep in Waterloo, they began their sight-seeing expedition on foot along the crooked roads, littered with stumps, rocks, swamps, and gullies, and small bridges made of trees laid sideways. They were greatly impressed with almost everything they saw on the walk, which extended several miles — the neat log homes, the livestock, the bountiful crops, and the quality of the wheat harvest that was nearing its end. They took particular enjoyment in meeting the residents and listening to their tragic histories of enslavement and to the triumphant stories of escape and freedom.[6]

Upon reaching the mission house known as Mount Hope on Saturday, August 28, they were welcomed by kindred spirits, missionaries John Brooks, originally from Massachusetts, and Fidelia Coburn from Maine. Miss Coburn had previously worked with Hiram Wilson at the British American Institute and both, like Wilson, continued to labour with the meagre support of the American Missionary Association, a few other anti-slavery societies, and the largesse of charitable donors, primarily from New England.

Mr. Brooks's home was comfortable and the nearby building where he preached and taught was described as "a noble school-house, fit for a church, or a large dwelling."[7] Miss Coburn lived and worked at her own mission, Mount Pleasant, about three miles away. That day, however, the two missionaries were together, Brooks having come to assist his female colleague who was becoming overwhelmed with the pressures of her situation. Reverend Young and Reverend Wilson sensed another reason, and advised the couple that it might be wise to get married, as they thought they "might be more useful."[8]

That evening, Samuel Young was called upon to share the story of Isaac Brown to a large gathering at Mount Hope. He was to preach the next morning at Mount Pleasant, but had to decline due to a severe headache. By afternoon it had subsided enough for him to fulfill that promise. The next day, Monday, August 30, he felt fit enough to speak for three hours to another large and responsive crowd. But he had overtaxed himself and an illness brought on by what they logically suspected was exhaustion started to overcome him.

By Tuesday evening, the two friends decided it best to begin their journey home. The twelve-mile walk from Waterloo to Mount Hope had only taken a few hours the week before, but the return trip was much slower. Two days were lost since Reverend Young was unable to travel. He was quickly losing strength as the strange malady took over. On Friday, September 3, they finally reached Waterloo, but could go no further and hired a room at Bowman's Tavern.

A doctor was summoned as soon as they arrived and he rushed to administer what medical treatment he could. By Monday, the patient was getting worse despite the care of a second, more accomplished doctor. Sensing that this might be an illness for which there was no cure,

Courtesy of Ellis Little Local History Room, Waterloo Public Library. Item ID: E-3-12.

Reverend Samuel Young spent his final days at Bowman's Tavern, also known as the "Farmer's Hotel." Although the original tavern burned to the ground in 1850, it was replaced by a similar structure pictured above.

Reverend Young grasped Hiram Wilson's hand and asked his friend not to leave him until he either recovered or was in his grave. He suffered with a burning fever and a debilitating headache that a cool cloth could relieve but little. The doctors were baffled as to how to treat him. On Wednesday, Young started to become delirious and increasingly unaware of his surroundings, symptoms that only became worse over the next four days. At dawn on Sunday morning, September 12, with Hiram Wilson at his side, as he had constantly been for six days, Samuel Young peacefully and silently took his final breath.

A panic had already set in among the people of the town, fearing contagion from whatever had claimed Young's life. Despite being physically and emotionally drained, Hiram Wilson rushed to find an owner of a horse and wagon, who would agree to carry the remains to Mount Hope for burial. Wilson judged that place to be most appropriate, lying in the black settlement where he had so recently shared the story of one of their fellows whom he had aided to freedom. By 5:00 p.m., Wilson had found a team and an open wagon to carry the coffin. A Danish man — who incidentally was exceedingly proud that the king of Denmark had moved to abolish slavery before the king of England — volunteered to act as teamster, and a black man, who had came from Mount Hope to check on Young's health, also agreed to accompany the body. This sombre entourage travelled seven miles until darkness overtook them. The living were offered lodging at the home of a Pennsylvania Deutch family, the dead was sheltered in the barn. Unbeknownst to all, a group of twenty-six black men upon first learning of Reverend Young's death left a campground meeting near Mount Hope at 3:00 a.m. to walk the fifteen miles to Waterloo to carry the corpse of the man they considered a hero to their race to the sacred ground where they buried their own loved ones.

The next morning the humble funeral cortege continued on. In the early afternoon, Hiram Wilson delivered the eulogy to a large black congregation that had travelled from across the Queen's Bush. The chosen Bible text was taken from the Book of Revelations: "Blessed are the dead that die in the Lord." All joined together to sing a song that Wilson had hastily written for the occasion:

Friend of the friendless and forlorn,
Kind brother to the bleeding slave,
Thy name we love — thy absence mourn,
We yield thee to the Martyr's grave.

Here on Mount Hope thy dust shall sleep.
Till the last trump of God shall sound,
Here round thy grave shall pilgrims weep,
And grateful tread this sacred ground.[9]

There was a gentle rain and many tears as they laid him to rest. Conspicuous among the mourners was the solitary figure of the black man who, along with Hiram Wilson, had brought the body to that place after having walked to Waterloo the day before with the intention of helping to attend to Samuel Young. Upon learning that he was dead, the man had become inconsolable. In Wilson's words "those scenes were solemn and impressive and will not soon be forgotten."[10]

Chapter Nine

But the Conflict Will Be Terrible

The conflict between the principle of liberty and the fact of slavery is coming gradually to an issue. Slavery has now the power, and falls into convulsions at the approach of freedom. That the fall of slavery is predetermined in the counsels of Omnipotence I cannot doubt; it is a part of the great moral improvement in the condition of man, attested by all the records of history. But the conflict will be terrible.[1]

— John Quincy Adams, December 13, 1838

With what they hoped was the most difficult period of their lives now behind them, Isaac and Susannah Brown attempted to settle into a normal life of relative anonymity. But it was exceedingly difficult to do so. Their story had captured the imagination of people in both Canada and the United States and the media of the times was reluctant to leave their story behind. The *Pennsylvania Freeman*, which was the weekly publication of the Pennsylvania Anti-Slavery Society, continued to express the optimism that the institution of slavery had been struck a mighty blow by the outcome of Isaac's case. The newspaper gave a lengthy report of the proceedings of the annual meeting of the Anti-Slavery Society of Eastern Pennsylvania, New Jersey, and Delaware, which included a segment on the profound and widespread indignation at the vile and dishonest tactics taken by the Grand Jury and the governor of Maryland in their attempt to retrieve Brown. The participants of the annual meeting believed that the conspiracy spoke volumes about the "demoralizing

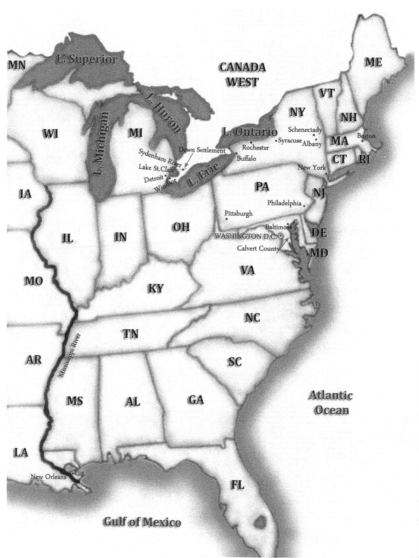

The cities identified on this map show the extent of Isaac Brown's travel during slavery and escape, including his ultimate flight to Canada.

Courtesy of Lori Gardner, Buxton National Historic Site & Museum.

effect of slavery" on even the most respected and prominent people when it came to this particular issue. They were also optimistic that northern officials would take heed of the admonitions that Pennsylvania authorities had been subjected to by a large number of citizens, who scolded them for not being firm enough in their stance against "the schemes of all men, who, under color of law are seeking to violate all law, human and devine." Most importantly, they believed that the message would spread across the entire South, that there was a growing anti-slavery sentiment in the north and that it "will not long submit to be trifled with, nor easily be imposed upon." Unable to resist a final word on the subject, and articulated in an almost un-Quaker-like manner, the committee expressed their great satisfaction at the discomfort of the "kidnappers" when they were thwarted in their attempt to take Brown and were forced to make a hasty retreat back to Maryland to escape going to prison themselves.[2]

Canadian newspapers were also drawn into publishing Brown's once tragic, but now feel-good story. After giving the details, the *Toronto Banner* asked its readers to spread the story to prevent any attempt to find a uniformed British North American magistrate who might, out of ignorance of the true facts, turn the fugitive over to Maryland agents.[3] The *Philadelphia Freeman*, always eager to publish more on Isaac Brown, learned of the Toronto publication and carried the *Banner's* article following its own editorial comment: "Should not the cheek of every American burn with shame at the disclosure of such facts as the following? A man seeking only his freedom, which no crime has forfeited, flies with the speed of terror from this 'free republic' this 'refuge for the oppressed of all nations,' and finds liberty and protection at the foot of the British throne! Well may the despots of the old world laugh to scorn our proud boasts of Freedom."[4]

Following the death of their friend and champion, Reverend Samuel Young, Brown's story was once again thrust under a more intense spotlight. The *Toronto Banner*, the *Globe*, the *True Wesleyan*, and *The New York Tribune* carried the melancholy news, adding that Isaac Brown and his family had joined the minister in Waterloo before he succumbed.[5] After learning about it in the *Public Ledger*, the *Pennsylvania Freeman* shared the news with its readers a week later in its October 7, 1847, edition. The *Toronto Mirror*, the *Christian World*, and the *Galt Reporter* also covered the story and *Christian*

World, *National Anti-Slavery Standard*, and the American Missionary Association asked the public to contribute any amount, however small, to the bereaved and impoverished widow and her now fatherless children.[6]

Death of Rev. Mr. Young.— In our last we mentioned that a minister of the gospel of this name, from the city of New York, had kindly accompanied the colored man, Brown, who had emancipated himself from bondage in order to lay his case before Lord Elgin. We regret to say that Mr. Young has fallen a victim to disease, which, we believe was caught on his way to Montreal, where he mixed much with the emigrants. Little more than two weeks ago, he was in Toronto, apparently in good health. He went to Waterloo the settlement of the colored population, along with the refugee and his family, where he was seized with the fatal disease which soon ended his life, and all his labours in this world.

There is something very affecting in the mode in which this faithful man has been cut down, and certainly he could not have fallen in a more noble cause. He was only about thirty years of age and a long career of usefulness in the Church was apparently before him. It please the great disposer of events to order it otherwise, and, we trust, to remove the departed to a higher sphere of service. Mr. Young has left a wife and seven children to lament his loss.

[Toronto Globe.]

We were well acquainted with brother Young and regret his fall. Ed. T.W.

From the True Wesleyan October 16, 1847

Boston's *Liberator* also carried the story on two different occasions and provided an additional heart-wrenching detail supplied by Hiram Wilson that had not appeared in other newspapers. When Wilson had returned to the Dawn Settlement following Reverend Young's burial, he found a letter that had arrived in his absence. Dated July 27 — the day before Young and the Brown's arrival at Dawn — the letter urged Young to return home to New York as quickly as possible as his wife was gravely ill and was not expected to recover. There was a very real fear that the couple's eight children would soon become orphans, if they were not already.[7]

Governor Thomas Pratt had a great deal of trouble trying to let go of his very public defeat in having Brown returned. At the conclusion of his very lengthy annual message to the General Assembly of Maryland, delivered on December 28 as the eventful year of 1847 came to its end, Pratt opined, "I wish, gentlemen, that I could close this communication without adverting to a subject, which it gives me great pain to be obliged to bring to your attention."[8] He proceeded to lament the several failed instances where Pennsylvania had refused to return runaway slaves to Maryland. He spoke with a special exasperation of the case of Isaac Brown, who Pratt felt was only held in the Philadelphia jail due to the threat of violence by the populace which would make it unsafe for Officer Zell to immediately attempt to return the fugitive to Maryland. The governor declared his frustration that Pennsylvania had defied the constitution of the United States with impunity.

Once on the subject, Pratt's ire very obviously began to boil. He reminded his listeners that slavery had existed for generations going back to colonial days when Great Britain sanctioned the practice and citizens had as much right over their slaves as they would over any other piece of property. But now, "this fanatical spirit" of abolitionists has destroyed the harmony that once existed among all of the States. In a prophetic tone, he warned that the issue was "of momentous importance, involving in its possible consequences the dissolution of the Union." Although Pratt appeared to have ignored his own counsel, he advised the Maryland House of Representatives and Senate that they should not approach the issue with anger, but rather appeal to the honour, the patriotism and the sense of justice of their counterparts in Pennsylvania to do the right thing which, to Pratt's mind, was "self evident."[9]

The *Pennsylvania Freeman* was quick to respond to the governor's speech, warning that all citizens should be vigilant and ensure that no attempts were made to weaken the anti-kidnapping law. All were encouraged to continue to agitate and to circulate petitions to let the legislature know that even stronger laws were needed.[10] Thomas Scarf, who years later wrote the monumental *History of Maryland*, had a very different view. In a bitter segment that appeared under the headline PENNSYLVANIA NULLIFYING THE CONSTITUTION, he wrote in unequivocal terminology that the case of Isaac Brown and other slaves who were not returned to Maryland changed the course of his state's history. The author argued that there was a public sentiment to gradually abolish slavery before those "outrages were committed." Following these acts, the mood changed in reaction to the "violent denunciations and improper interference" by "fanatical" Northern abolitionists. To be certain that his message was clear, Scarf repeated that the blame rested squarely on the shoulders of those abolitionists for preventing the end of the institution of slavery.[11]

Lucretia Mott, the diminutive Quaker and human rights advocate whose place in history rivals that of any of the giants of her time, found no common ground with Thomas Scarf or Governor Pratt on that issue. She and her fellow anti-slavery companions remained firmly committed to their cause. They took great satisfaction in their recent success, but were extremely careful in committing details to paper that might incriminate themselves or reveal specifics of their Underground Railroad operations that might prevent using the same tactics to help fugitives in the future. However, Mott relished the thought that eventually those remarkably stories could be triumphantly shared: "Isaac Brown's & others not a few, will tell well in history, some time hence, "in the days of freedom, oh"!"[12]

Chapter Ten

Many Thousand Gone

No more driver's lash for me
No more, no more
No more driver's lash for me,
Many thousand gone.

— Traditional

In the first few months of freedom as the decade of the 1840s drew to a close, news of the Brown family quietly subsided from newspaper pages, as well as from the private correspondence of the abolitionists who had taken such an interest in their case. After all, there were hundreds, even thousands, of others who had the resolve and the opportunity to flee that required their immediate attention and their help. Even those numbers were a only a small percentage of the more than 3 million souls still firmly held within slavery's grasp. They were part of the much larger struggle that could never be forgotten. And, of course, there were untold others of different races who were worthy of the sympathy of others. Included in that number were Samuel Young's children and his widow, who had almost miraculously survived her illness. According to a notice that appeared in the October 22, 1847, edition of the *Liberator*, a considerable amount of money had been raised and forwarded to her.

Whether it was by a desire for anonymity to stay out of the public record or just the loss of official and private documents over a century and a half, details about Isaac Brown, Susannah, and their children's first months in Canada remain elusive. Could uncertainty and fear have caused them to have taken on yet another alias as did so many others? Could they simply have been missed when the census taker or tax officials went about their business recording residents? Did their anti-slavery friends scattered across the north become more cautious when sharing information in the written form? Isaac Brown could certainly attest to the potential disastrous results from revealing too much in that format. Could he have been the solitary figure who walked from the Queen's Bush to Waterloo to give comfort to Samuel Young during the latter's final illness and was inconsolable upon learning of his death?

So many unanswered and now unanswerable questions surround that period of the Browns' lives. But questions such as to where would they settle — which are only an intriguing curiosity for twenty-first-century researchers — demanded more immediate answers for the family. As would be expected, it was clearly difficult for this, or for any other, penniless family to establish themselves in a new land. There were plentiful

This map shows the areas in Canada West surrounded by the largest black populations in the antebellum period.

choices throughout Canada West, which was the fugitive's favoured destination in the British North American provinces. Among these options were the growing cities of Toronto and Hamilton, Essex County's Colchester, Amherstburg, Sandwich, Windsor, and Drummondville, and St. Catharines in the Niagara Peninsula. Places that were farther into the interior of the province like London, Oro, Norwich, Owen Sound, and dozens of other places, offered a geographic as well as a psychological cushion from the United States border and would-be slave catchers who had the audacity to attempt a foreign kidnapping.

The long-established Dawn Settlement, where the Browns had spent their first night together in a Canadian home originally appeared to be the most obvious place in which the family should establish themselves. But it was not to be. Shortage of funds, internal bickering, whispered complaints from within, and persistent public criticism from without plagued the institute and its managers. Despite years of self-sacrifice and humanitarian service to the downtrodden, Hiram Wilson, the Brown family's first Canadian friend, was a constant target for criticism because of his never-ending appeals for money, for his shared part in mismanaging the business of the settlement, and for the overall disappointment in not realizing the possibilities that Dawn once promised.[1]

One of the trustees of the British American Institute at Dawn claimed that the decline at the institution began (at about the same time as the Brown family's arrival) immediately following the death of Hiram's wife Hannah, who was described as "a friend who could never be replaced" and as one who "was a mother and a teacher" to all who abided there.[2] Even Lewis Tappan, an old friend and financial supporter, added insult to injury informing the missionary that "I have made up my mind, dear brother, that you are not a suitable man to be at the head of an enterprise ... that much money has been wasted at Dawn Mills that the scheme was an injudicious one.... You have not sufficient judgment or financial skill for such an enterprise.... As a preacher I learn that you are not acceptable to the colored people, lacking animation, vivacity & free utterance." With a less than feeble attempt at comforting Wilson, Tappan added, "I think you will not be displeased at my telling you my opinion in this friendly way."[3]

The widowed, beleaguered, and humiliated Wilson's spirits were somewhat buoyed when he was soon smitten by Mary Ann Holland, whom he described as "one of the most excellent of the daughters of New England."[4] The couple married in early summer of 1848, giving Wilson a companion, a mother for his children, and an assistant in his anti-slavery labours. But his personal financial situation continued to be grave. His commitment to the black refugees was so demanding that he could find little time to devote to farming his land and raising his family. Mounting debts forced him to sell his horse, which was his only means of conveyance, and he feared that he would soon have to sell his house, realities that would certainly suggest that the house that the Brown family first inhabited on Wilson's land was only a short-term home.[5] Furthermore, Wilson relinquished his role as manager of the British American Institute, criticized the current management, expressed his disappointment in the effectiveness of the manual labour school that he superintended, and felt that the burden was such that he would soon have to leave Dawn in particular and perhaps the missionary field to the fugitives in general.[6] It was not until November 1850, when, after many months of anguished vacillation, prayer, complaints, appeals, and introspection, Wilson finally moved to St. Catharines, where he resumed his calling.

The Queen's Bush, although also safely in the interior of the province and possessing the Brown's emotional tie to the final resting place of Samuel Young, was gradually becoming a less attractive destination as many of the early black inhabitants were moving away — driven out by the inability to pay for the Clergy Reserve lands that they had settled on, cleared and cultivated, all without having paid for, thus not having clear title to the properties. In 1791, the British Constitutional Act set aside these large parcels of land for the use of the Protestant church and clergy, specifically those of the Church of England. Decades later, much of these lands in Upper and Lower Canada still sat vacant and irresistibly lured impoverished pioneers to cut a home and a farm out of the timbered wilderness. After years of dispute as to the use of the land, the government finally decided to make it legally available for settlement. By the latter 1840s, when the surveyors were mapping out the lots

— at about the same time that the Brown family was deciding where to establish their homestead — the black community of Queen's Bush was irrevocably changing. Even John Brooks and his recent bride Fidelia Coburn Brooks were about to move on to new missionary endeavours in Sierra Leone, Africa.[7]

The Browns would have learned that many of the inhabitants of the Queen's Bush moved north to Owen Sound on the shores of Georgian Bay, tempted by land grants of fifty acres. Others were drawn south-westerly to the newly formed Elgin Settlement and Buxton Mission, an all-black colony in Kent County, where land was fertile and affordable and the climate somewhat more moderate. Opportunities were arising there for a variety of occupations and there was a prevailing optimism of building a community among others of similar background and complexion.

Buxton, as the settlement was commonly called, was comprised of nearly nine thousand acres of contiguous virgin Clergy Reserves and Crown lands that were purchased from the government by a large group of Canadian anti-slavery philanthropists known as the Elgin Association. This group, as well as the settlement itself, was directed by Reverend William King, a white Presbyterian minister of Irish birth who had immigrated to the area near where Isaac Brown was once exiled in Louisiana in the American South. He married into a slave-holding family, and, through inheritance and purchase, became the owner of fifteen slaves. Reverend King, a man of evolving and practical moral principles, became increasingly opposed to slavery, but, because of Louisiana law, could not legally emancipate his chattel within that state. Thus, he removed his slaves to Canada where they could live as free people, and established a settlement for them and for other former slaves as well as free blacks, a place where they could become masters of their own destiny.

The land, which had a gentle descending northerly slope from Lake Erie toward the Thames River, was surveyed into fifty-acre lots and made available at the modest price of $2.50 an acre with a ten-year repayment term. Extensive coverage in North American and British newspapers and in anti-slavery circles brought a great deal of positive attention to the settlement, and within a decade over one thousand runaways and free men came and took up residence there. Several thousand additional uninhabited acres surrounding the settlement attracted hundreds more blacks who wished to have an emotional, social, and physical tie to this grand undertaking. Isaac Brown would eventually be in that group, but not for another decade after his arrival in Canada.

Positioned on the banks of the River Thames, halfway between the Dawn and Elgin Settlements and still within the confines of Kent County, was the town of Chatham. The *Voice of the Fugitive* newspaper reported that in the mid-nineteenth century the population was 2,070, living in both frame and brick homes. They belonged to "congregations of all the leading Christian denominations" and the town had:

> [S]everal good schools, a circulating library, six Divines, six Physicians, six Lawyers, three deputy Provincial Surveyors, three Apothecaries, Merchants' shops and stores beyond number: there are two Machine shops and Steam Engine factories, two Iron and Brass Foundries. There are ten Steam Engines in active operation in different establishments, five Flour and Grist Mill, and two more being erected. Three first class Steam Boats belong to the port, with several of the finest Sail Vessels upon the Lakes.

Proving that there was something for everyone, the article continued to boast that "there are three Breweries, each manufacturing choice specimens of that delicious beverage called Beer, three Distilleries of Whiskey and one Tobacco Manufactory." Apparently fighting an uphill battle were "two Lodges belonging to The Sons of Temperance." Rounding out the description were "two Brick Yards, and Mechanics' Artisans, &c., of every useful description."[8]

In the 1850s, approximately one-third of Chatham's population was of African descent and the newly incorporated town received effusive praise as a destination for fugitives.[9] The *Frederick Douglass' Paper* proclaimed that it was "'a blessed city of refuge' for the down-trodden ... It is Liberia of the North, provided by Heaven for the fugitive." The same article notes that the black residents "are prosperous and happy" and "whenever a fugitive arrives, he meets a joyous welcome, and at once finds employment and good support."[10] Another visitor noted that despite bitter prejudice, he "found colored men prosecuting the various fundamental handicrafts of civilized life. I found them carpenters, blacksmiths, cabinet makers, shoemakers, &c., without let or hindrance."[11] Isaac Brown would also soon be counted in that number, but not for a while yet.

For whatever reason, it was not until four years after his arrival in Canada that this same middle-aged runaway slave from Maryland resurfaced in the public record. No longer front-page news, a small article that was almost buried on the second page of the November 5, 1851, edition of the *Voice of the Fugitive* newspaper showed that the family had not been totally forgotten by their friends:

> We would acknowledge with gratitude the reception of $20, from our antislavery friends in Wilmington, Pa., transmitted by our excellent friends James and Lucretia Mott, for the relief of suffering fugitive-$5 of which we have already conveyed to Samuel Russell and family, according to order.

Chapter Eleven

Something to Hope For

Most interesting of all, are the inhabitants. Twenty years ago, most of them were slaves, who owned nothing, not even their children. Now they own themselves; they own their houses and farms; and they have their wives and their children about them. They have the great essentials for human happiness; something to love, something to do, and something to hope for.[1]

— Samuel Gridley Howe, Boston, 1863

Somewhat surprisingly, as the newspaper article suggested, Isaac Brown chose to permanently adopt the name "Samuel Russell" that he had assumed after his successful flight from slavery. Surprising, considering that this alias was widely known after having been revealed in Philadelphia courtrooms and printed in dozens of newspaper articles. Anyone who might still be doggedly pursuing him would not be fooled by this transparent change. Other runaways changed their names multiple times in the attempt to erase any tracks they may have inadvertently left behind. Some of those later reverted to their original name after the emotional intensity of their experience subsided somewhat and they began to breathe a bit easier as they adjusted to their new reality. The decision that Isaac made had to be enormously difficult — relinquishing the name that he had been known by for most of a lifetime, the name that his parents, siblings, and many kinsmen carried in Calvert County. And of course, "Brown" was the surname of his wife and his many children.

On the other hand, perhaps making the choice may have been less monumental than one might think. After all, it was part of Isaac's own self-assertion and reconstruction as a new man, as his own man. However, despite whatever internal conflicts may have come into play, the patriarch of the family shed both his Christian and his family name. His immediate family took a less dramatic compromise; Susannah Brown became Susannah Russell and their children — from twenty-year-old Lucinda to baby Rebecca — likewise adopted the surname Russell.

The older children would have been able to find work in the surrounding fields or as common labourers or house servants and contribute to the family's finances, thereby freeing them from the humiliation of having to depend upon the largesse of others. This would help distance them from the raging controversy called "the begging system" that split the black Canadian population, many of whom proudly wanted to proclaim to a doubtful world that they were perfectly capable of being independent and self-reliant once given the chance.

The Brown — now Russell — children would also quickly reach the age where they could start out on their own and begin their own families. Lucinda was first when Wesleyan Methodist minister, Reverend Samuel Fear, after publishing banns inquiring if anyone knew of any impediment to her proposed nuptials, joined her in marriage to Richard Nevils on August 30, 1849.[2] It is documentation of Lucinda's wedding that gives the first real hint of where the Russell family lived after leaving Dawn. The ceremony took place in Harwich Township, which partially surrounded the town of Chatham to the southeast. It is interesting to note that although the bride and the two witnesses, Jason Grant and Mary Jane Gibson, were black, the Nevils family, who were of Irish descent, were white.

The couple were no doubt the target of a great deal of criticism because, at the time of their wedding, Chatham was notorious for its racial divisions, and, due to the pending prospect of a large number of blacks moving into the nearby Buxton Settlement, feelings were reaching a fever pitch. Despite flowery references by visitors to the town, the welcome mat was not laid out for blacks who sought to make Chatham their home. Intermarriage would have certainly have raised an outcry. The widespread anti-black movement was led by Edwin Larwill, a

Courtesy of Buxton National Historic Site & Museum.

In his 1855 Autobiography of a Fugitive Negro: His Anti-Slavery Labours in the United States, Canada, & England, *Samuel Ringgold Ward, a travelling lecturer for the Anti-Slavery Society of Canada, gave his thoughts on Edwin Larwill (shown above) and on the behaviour of some Chatham residents towards him (see full quote in Chapter 11 notes): "I must be allowed to express my regret that some of the black men of Chatham — men, too, of wealth and position, as compared with many others, white and black — are wanting in manliness. They do not bravely, manfully, stand up for themselves and their people as they should. They cower before the brawling demagogue Larwill — a man well known as an enemy of the Negro, but a man beneath any manly Negro's contempt — a recreant Englishman, of low origin but aspiring tendencies, not knowing his place, and consequently not keeping it."[3]*

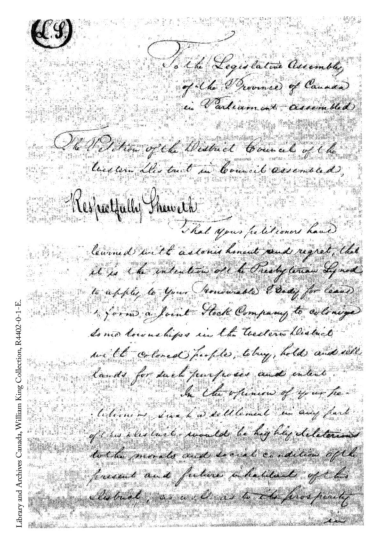

The petition sent to the Legislative Assembly of Canada, February 19, 1849, protested the settlement of Blacks in the district on the grounds that it "would be highly deleterious to the morals and social condition of the present and future inhabitants."

local politician, newspaper editor, and tinsmith, who, along with other prominent men, organized meetings, wrote newspaper articles, posted handbills, and circulated petitions to protest the further introduction of blacks into parts of the province where whites already lived.

One such petition, addressed to the Presbyterian Synod and signed by three hundred citizens, who, on the one hand, professed that they "will not for one moment question the pure and Philanthropic Motives which have prompted you to step forward and assist in ameliorating and improving the condition of the Colored Man, as men, we have no objection to their enjoying every privilege and Rights, Religious, Moral, Political, and Social ..." but on the other, explicitly spelled out their true feelings:

> The Negro is a distinct species of the Human Family and, in the opinion of your Memorialists is far inferior to that of the European. Let each link in the great Scale of existence have its place; the white man was never intended to be linked with the black. Amalgamation is as disgusting to the Eye, as it is immoral in its tendencies and all good men will discountenance it.[4]

Despite this poisoned atmosphere, Lucinda and Richard Nevils braved the opposition, taking comfort in the company of Chatham's black community whose numbers would soon increase dramatically following the passage of the Fugitive Slave Act of 1850 when thousands of American refugees, both runaways as well as legitimately free, fled to Canada. They came to escape the terror of that law whose terms mandated the return of fugitives who had fled to any part of the union, demanded that ordinary citizens participate in their capture, and refused the right for blacks to testify in their own defence. In effect, officials were encouraged to disregard the kidnapping of free blacks who were destined to be sent to the South as slaves.

The passage of that law removed any thought that might have lingered for Lucinda's father to ever return to the country of his youth. Despite dogged unsuccessful attempts to pinpoint the exact location of the entire Russell family during their first few years in Canada, given the location of Lucinda's wedding, it is probably safe to assume that they lived in or around Chatham. Proof positive does not appear until eight years later, when, in the summer of 1855, the name Samuel Russell prominently appeared in the *Provincial Freeman*, an abolitionist newspaper that had just moved from Toronto and resumed publication in Chatham.

It appeared that Samuel had begun to prosper, and, being in the healing profession, was no doubt a respected member of the community.

DR. SAMUEL RUSSELL,
BOTANIC MEDICINES.
RAPID CURES, AND LOW CHARGES!

Charity's Brick Buildings, next door to the " Freeman" Office, King Street East,
CHATHAM, C. W.
August 20, 1855.   18-1y

Courtesy of Edward and Maxine Robbins.

Samuel Russell regularly advertised his medical practice in the Provincial Freeman. *This ad is from the September 15, 1855, edition.*

Courtesy of Chatham Kent Museum.

he Charity Building in Chatham, which housed the medical practice of Doctor Samuel Russell and the offices of the Provincial Freeman *newspaper, as it looked in the mid-nineteenth century.*

His office was in the impressive red brick Charity Building on the southeast corner of King and Adelaide Streets. It was owned by James Charity, a shoemaker who kept upper-floor apartments that could be reached by staircases in the rear of the building. The ground floor was divided into four shops, with Charity's shoe store facing the street corner. The two adjoining offices of Mary Ann Shadd and her brother Isaac, one of which they used for their *Provincial Freeman* newspaper and the other for their printing presses, were on the opposite side of the building. In the centre of the structure was Dr. Russell's office, identified for passersby with a hanging sign in the front and a green curtain stretched across the window for privacy.[5]

Samuel Russell was commonly known by occupation as a "root doctor." These practitioners were common in the South where roots, herbs, and various folk treatments were plentiful, but scientifically trained doctors were not. Perhaps in the "Negro quarters" in Calvert County, Maryland, a younger Isaac Brown had been instructed, or least observed which plants to use to cure certain ailments. Perhaps the tradition had been passed down from African ancestors, or learned from Native Americans, or simply came into common usage by trial and error and necessity. Whatever the genesis of his interest in this vocation, by the time he set up his own practice he was a disciple of Samuel Thomson, who had developed a popular method of medical practice. He published numerous volumes as well as revisions and additions to introduce devotees to his theories and practices, including a work on anatomy, recognition and treatment of diseases, and sections on botany. Thomson had numerous travelling agents who sold the patent for his work, as well as the natural products such as cayenne peppers, hemlock, mustard, ginseng, red clover, turpentine, ginger root, and the exotic-sounding Balm of Gilead for use in treating patients.

Before plying his new trade, Samuel Russell would have to subscribe to the theory that "all diseases originate from ... the deranged state of fluids in the body, by the absence of heat, or loss of vitality; which produces an over pressure or excess of circulation to the head, and a proportionate deficiency in the feet. This creates derangement in the organs of sense, and a proportionate want of action with the digestive apparatus."

Courtesy of Lloyd Library and Museum, Cincinnati, Ohio.

In order to qualify to practise the Thomsonian system of medicine, Samuel Russell would have to pay his fee, whereupon he would have received a similar certificate as pictured above.

Although there were many different medicines recommended for various ailments, no matter what the disease, the Thomson physicians were to always begin their treatment by "Equalizing the Circulation":

> In the first place, put the feet of the patient into water as hot as can be borne, increase the heat by adding water of a higher temperature until a copious perspiration is started on the forehead and in the palms of the hands; the patient may be in the bath if thought necessary; this will afford some relief. Then take brown emetic, cayenne, composition, and nerve powder, of each one teaspoonful, put them into one pint of boiling water and let them steep for ten minutes; sweeten with molasses, and let half the quantity be given as an injection, as hot as it can be borne, and let the patient retain it as long as possible. This will turn the excitement from the head downwards and sickness at the stomach will be produced. Then give a table spoonful of the tincture of lobelia and a small quantity of cayenne, in some simple tea, and if this does not

produce sufficient vomiting repeat the dose. The vomiting will be easy, the veins in the hands and feet will be filled, the head, in consequence of the equalization of the circulation, will be relieved, and the whole system will become quiet and easy.[6]

On October 12, 1855, within weeks of his advertisement first appearing in the newspaper, Samuel Russell "root doctor" and his wife Susannah purchased a home and small lot, thirty-two feet wide by one hundred feet deep, on the southwest corner of King and Adelaide, directly across the street from his place of business. The couple bought their new home from local carpenter John Fleming and wife Mary, for 178 pounds, fifteen shillings. The Flemings agreed to hold the mortgage for the full amount with the ambitious repayment schedule to be thirty-seven pounds, ten shillings on December 1, 1855, another thirty-seven pounds, ten shillings April 1, 1856, fifty pounds on October 12, 1856, and the final fifty-three pounds, fifteen shillings on October 12, 1857. In order to make the transaction official — just as he had done in 1847 when the fugitive slave Isaac Brown gave his statement to a Pennsylvania court — Samuel Russell, even though he was perfectly capable of doing otherwise, signed the document with an X.

This signature appears on documents identified as being in Book B, Folio 497, registration numbers 566 and 567 are microfilmed at the Chatham Kent Registry Office. The property is part of Lot 74, Old Survey, Town of Chatham.

Chapter Twelve

I Can Do My Own Thinkings

*I had rather live in Canada, on one potato a day, than to
live in the South with all the wealth they have got. I am
now my own mistress, and need not work when I am sick. I
can do my own thinkings, without having any one to think
for me, — to tell me when to come, what to do, and to sell
me when they get ready. I wish I could have my relatives
here. I might say a great deal more against slavery — nothing for it.*[1]

— Mrs. Christopher Hamilton

Life must have been exciting and eventful as the family settled into
their new situation in 1855. They now lived and worked within the
bustling centre of the African-Canadian community in the east end
of Chatham. Lucinda's twenty-year-old younger sister, Catharine, also
lived in nearby Harwich Township, having married a man named Berry.
Catharine had married young and soon presented her parents with a
granddaughter, Mary, who was now four. Leonard Russell, who had just
turned twenty and was the oldest of the boys that came to Canada with
the family, appears to have been the most independent of the siblings
and spent most of his adulthood in neighbouring Essex County and in
Michigan. Fourteen-year-old Jacob, who remained with the family, had
not been able to attend school and even by age twenty had not learned
to read or write, probably having had to spend his youth working to help
support his family.

Perhaps also contributing to the missed opportunity was the fact that the black children were not allowed to attend the publicly funded government schools that had white students, even though their parents were taxed like anyone else to build and support them. In many parts of the county, indeed in the province, that fact, and the absence of a separate coloured school within a reasonable distance, eliminated the option for many children to enroll. Black children in Chatham had little choice other than go to what Mary Ann Shadd described in the *Provincial Freeman* as "that disgrace of the place the little colored school house" that "should be left to rot down, or to stand as it is a monument of the injustice the colored people sustain."[2] Although supported by government funds, the school was clearly inadequate, short of basic teaching materials, and always overcrowded.[3] By 1856, eighty children were enrolled, but average attendance was only fifty-five.[4] Many other eligible children had to be turned away for lack of room.

Poverty was an enduring issue in most of the black communities, including Chatham, and missionaries regularly mentioned that some children could not attend school for want of proper clothing.[5] In addition to that, parents had to pay to send their children to that school unless they were "poor widows and other respectable, but destitute persons, really in need of some aid."[6] The costs for admission, however small, would have been problematic for the financially beleaguered Russell family in those early days.

The younger children, including William, twelve, and Nancy, eleven, were more fortunate when it came to educational opportunity. Unfortunately, the names of three of their other siblings — sisters, ages thirteen and seven, and brother, age five — were not recorded, but presumably they too would have attended school. As the decade went by, a Mission School was established in a more suitable building through the initiative of Mary Ann Shadd (who, in 1856, married and became Mary Ann Shadd Cary), her brother Isaac and his wife Amelia with the support of New England philanthropists, the British Colonial Church and School Society, and the American Missionary Association.[7] The children were taught a classical education that consisted of algebra, arithmetic, history, philosophy, grammar, geography, and penmanship, as well

Courtesy of Buxton National Historic Site & Museum.

Courtesy of Buxton National Historic Site & Museum.

Left: *After removing her printing presses from the office building that she shared with Samuel Russell in the summer or fall of 1856, Mary Ann Shadd Cary and her brother Isaac continued to publish the* Provincial Freeman *for another three years. However, it appeared sporadically at times, sometime with long lapses.*

Right: *Although less well-known than his famous sister, Isaac D. Shadd was also a remarkable figure. In 1858, he was arrested as one of the leaders of the Chatham Vigilance Committee for storming a train and rescuing a boy who was being carried back to slavery.*

as a class that would have been dear to their father's heart — botany. In addition to those courses, the more artistic endeavours of music, singing, and painting were also offered. William was becoming a particularly accomplished student. His parents no doubt swelled with pride when his name appeared in North America's foremost anti-slavery newspaper, Boston's *Liberator*, after taking second prize for proficiency in history.[8]

Chatham was entering a period of rapid change and growth. Isaac Shadd reported that many of the old and dilapidated stores and buildings had been torn down and replaced with large and impressive new buildings, many of which were three or four storeys high, boasting pillars, and door and window sills made of iron. Minor things like four-paned windows that replaced the old-style twelve-paned ones, and oil-filled lamps that took the place of tallow candles were a more subtle improvement. On a grander scale, there were many new businesses facing the plank roads that stretched in all directions, replacing roads that turned to mud during times of inclement weather. Sewers were being buried along King Street, and the road itself was the first to be "macadamized" — the process of covering it with crushed stones, small enough to knead together so as to allow easy passage for wagon wheels and to avoid causing problems for horses' hooves. In the spring, the Thames was filled with steamboats and lake vessels, adding a scenic vitality to the atmosphere. New bridges over the river and McGregor's Creek were being constructed, encouraging commerce and social interaction.[9]

The black population was also steadily increasing, so much so that a female resident of the town quipped "at Chatham, the fugitives are as thick as blackbirds in a cornfield." The town regularly drew the attention of the outside world, both black and white. In 1855, Benjamin Drew, a Boston abolitionist, visited many of the black settlements in Canada West, interviewing former slaves. He published many of them the following year, in an invaluable work, *The Refugee: or the Narratives of Fugitive Slaves in Canada.* Of Chatham, he wrote:

> Here, indeed, more fully than anywhere else, the traveller realizes the extent of the American exodus. At every turn, he meets members of the African race, single or in groups; he sees them building and painting houses, working in mills, engaged in every handicraft employment: here he notices a street occupied by colored shop-keepers and clerks: if he steps into the environs, he finds blacks in every quarter, busy upon their gardens and farms.[10]

Drew was impressed to learn that a self-help committee, known as "True Band," had recently been formed with over 375 members. Among their many goals was to improve all schools and encourage all children to be

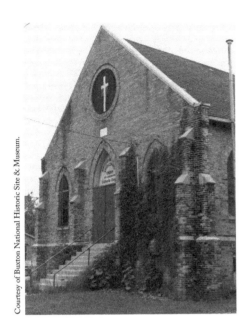

Courtesy of Buxton National Historic Site & Museum.

Victoria Chapel of British Methodist Episcopal Church, Chatham, where Samuel Russell and family attended services.

formally educated; to eliminate prejudice; to stop the widespread begging system where agents insinuated the helplessness of blacks in Canada and appealed to them for financial aid; to eliminate litigation by settling disputes through a committee; to raise funds to care for the sick, the poor and for newly arrived fugitives; and to bring all of the churches together.[11]

The churches were a vital part of the community's spiritual, educational, and social lives. While the majority of blacks were either Baptist or Methodist, others were Anglican, Presbyterian, or Roman Catholic. Samuel Russell and his family attended the British Methodist Episcopal (BME) Church — known as Victoria Chapel — which had the distinction of being the edifice in which many of the Canadian African Methodist Episcopal (AME) churches split away from their American counterparts and renamed their churches in honour of the country that had given them true freedom. The newly constructed Victoria Chapel was impressive and a Chatham newspaper editor described it thusly: "In point of size and exterior and interior finish, it will compare very favourably with any house for public worship in Chatham. It is large, and its fittings are complete in every point; nay, more, they are a credit not only to the spirit of the pastor and congregation, but to the mechanics who performed the workmanship."[12] Presumably the Russell family would have been among the large congregation that filled the chapel, overflowed into the doorways, and, from outside, strained to hear through open windows the first official service of the new conference one autumn Sunday morning in 1856.[13]

Beside the many events that took place in the church, there were many other organizations and social activities available for all members of the Russell family. There was a Temperance Society, Prince Hall Masonic Lodge, a band, a glee club, and a debating society.[14] Showing that they had not forgotten their past, there was a vigilance committee and an anti-slavery society. On one occasion, over one hundred citizens stormed a train and made a dangerous and dramatic rescue of a young boy, travelling with man who claimed to be his master who was returning him to their home in the South.[15]

Summer evenings were special times. One white man recalled that as a boy he was captivated listening to the former slaves who sat beneath towering maple trees singing spirituals and folk songs in harmony:

> [P]ouring out the sorrow and grief of slave years, the loves and losses, the solace found in music that lifted not only themselves but all who heard above the mundane and sordid....To hear "Swing Low, Sweet Chariot" carried by a clear, pure soprano, with the thrumming harmony of a group swelling to the chorus one could almost see, as surely the singers did, the celestial vision of it, and feel like dodging at the low-swinging of its golden steeds and wheels. To hear the finest basso Chatham ever had sing Rocked in the Cradle of the Deep, or The Sexton's Song with its "I gather them in", was spine tingling.[16]

The same writer had special memories of hiding in the shadows and watching the annual "Camp Meetings" held by the black churches in McGregor's bush near the Russells' home. These were grand events with booths that sold fried chicken and catfish, roast corn, Johnny cake, and pop. A hollow stump served as a pulpit for the ministers and logs were arranged in a semi-circle for seats for the audience. At nightfall, a large fire was lit to illuminate the scene and the minister would begin a fire-and-brimstone sermon, at times so powerful that some of the congregation dropped to their knees to repent their sins. Others were so overcome that they fell and rolled on the ground.

The Russells no doubt were among those festive and devoted crowds. They also probably joined many of those same neighbours in the merriment that swept across Chatham early one June morning in 1856 when their arch enemy, Edwin Larwill, was hanged by the neck in effigy from a tree on a downtown street. The editors of the *Provincial Freeman* had great fun describing the member of Parliament's "*lofty* position, with feet occupying the position the head generally do." After referencing that his feet were resting on the wind, they relished informing their readers that upon looking at his face it was difficult to determine whether or not it belonged to a "'Negro, Quadroon, Mulatto, Samboe, Half-bred, Mule, Mongrel or Conglomerate;' but had we have seen his ears, we might have supposed him to have been a Donkey." In a final triumphant swipe, the author of the article asked that the tree be cut down and preserved as a remembrance of the auspicious event. The article appeared under the rhetorical heading WHO WILL WEEP?[17] Later that same year, the black community dealt Larwill an even more serious blow when many of the county's black males came together to cast their vote in the provincial election. They voted en masse for the competing candidate Archie McKellar, who had been a staunch advocate of their rights, thereby soundly defeating their long-time foe.

Chapter Thirteen

The River Jordan Is Muddy and Cold

The river Jordan is muddy and cold
Well it chills the body but not the soul
All my trials Lord soon be over

— Traditional, arranged by Peter Webster

In 1857, Samuel Russell decided to make a major move. His medical practice was not as lucrative as he had hoped and it was difficult to meet his obligation of paying the mortgage on his Chatham home. The total amount of 178 pounds, fifteen shillings, was to be paid in full by October of that year. With twenty shillings in a pound, that meant that he owed 3,575 shillings altogether. Even if the children contributed, it was an almost impossible task. Sixteen-year-old Jacob and older brother Leonard were common labourers who could only earn from six to eight shillings per day, and there was never a guarantee on how many days they could work. If they found seasonal work with a farmer outside of town and had to board, their pay would only be a little over three shillings per day. If they found a permanent job as a household servant, they might receive seventy shillings for a month's work. Lucinda and Catharine had their own households to concern themselves with and could ill afford to support their birth family. Even on days that William, Nancy, and their slightly older sister may have taken off school and found an odd job, at their age they could only expect to make one shilling and ten pence (twelve pence in a shilling).

Some people were now using dollars instead of the old British currency, where 35.5 shillings was the equivalent of one United States dollar, but no matter, expenses always seemed to exceed income.[1] Samuel's medical practice faced stiff competition from the other black doctors in the area, all of whom appeared to enjoy a higher status in the community. Money was also tight with many would-be patients. Even his office-building mates at the *Provincial Freeman* constantly struggled financially and even advertised that they would accept produce in lieu of cash.

With financial calamity looming, the Russells had only to look for possible relief a few short miles away, to the large unsettled Crown lands known as the Raleigh Plains, just west of Chatham and south of the Thames River. The banks of the Thames were long-settled by United Empire Loyalist families who had been granted land in the latter part of the eighteenth century following the American Revolution. Some of them had brought their slaves with them at the time when slavery was still legal in this British colony. After slavery was abolished in 1834, some of them remained and lived among those Loyalists and their descendants, which included the family of Captain John Drake who had been involved in the transatlantic slave trade from the Guinea coast of Africa to the New World before the trade was outlawed in 1807.[2]

Courtesy of Chatham Kent Museum.

A view of King Street in Chatham as it looked in the 1850s.

The Raleigh Plains were also immediately north of the Buxton Settlement. Three thousand of these acres had, in fact, been offered to Reverend William King and the Elgin Association. The practical decision was made not to purchase them because most of it was low-lying marsh and they believed it would present an almost impossible challenge to make the land fit for agriculture. However, they underestimated the resolve of the black pioneers, used to surviving on very little and eager to have something more. A group of those hardy individuals moved into the marsh and dug ditches by hand to drain the surface water away. Soon, houses were erected in the drier clearings and crops were planted into what was becoming some of the richest soil in the township. Barns and fences were built to house and secure their pigs, chickens, and cows. Horses, rather than oxen, were the primary beasts of burden and means of transportation and every family hoped to have at least one in their stable.

Samuel Russell joined the group of families who took possession of some of this land that no one else had any interest in at the time. The two-hundred-acre farm that the Russells selected was on the most westerly border of Raleigh Township in what had been surveyed and identified as Lot 1, Concession 4. When the tax collector made his annual trip throughout the township to assess each individual property, he scarcely knew what to do with this extended, all-black settlement of "squatters" that stretched up and down the area. He noted that Dr. Samuel Russell's large farm was worth only fifteen pounds. By comparison, farms that were half that size on slightly higher ground within a few miles were worth ten times as much.[3] Because of the relative worthlessness of the land, Russell was only assessed one pence for his share of supporting the "lunatic asylum" and four pence for general school taxes. Added to that was one shilling, seven pence for Kent County taxes and four pence for Raleigh Township taxes. The assessor noted that Samuel Russell had "no goods" and assessed him a total of two shillings, four pence. Despite the fact that his taxes were relatively inexpensive — less than one day's pay for a common labourer — Russell, along with several of his neighbours who were also squatters, was listed on the page of the tax assessor's ledger with the heading: "List of the Uncollected Rates on the Collectors Rolls for the Township of Raleigh for the Year 1857."[4]

| 1 | 2 | 3 | 4 | REAL PROPERTY | | | ASSESSED VALUE & AMOU | | |
No.	NAMES OF PARTIES ASSESSED.	Freeholders.	Householders.	5 No. of Concession, Street, Square, or other designation	6 No. of Lot, part Lot, or House.	7 No. of Acres, Superficial Feet, or other Measurement.	8 Value of Real Property.	9 Am't of taxable & Personal Property or Income.	10 Total Real and Personal Proper...
	Coloured Men Squatters								
600	Samuel Russell Dr.	1	4		1	200	15	"	1
601	Edward Brown	1	"		2	200	15	.	1
602	Henry Spencer	1	"		3	200	15	"	1
603	Daniel Johnson	1	"		4	200	15	"	1
604	George Snively	1	"	n.½.	6	100	8	"	
605	Robert Eloney	1	"	s.½.	7	100	8	"	
606	Charles Decant	1	5		1	50	10	"	1
607	Daniel Gooden See page 62 &63	1	"	s.½.	3	100	18	"	1
608	Samuel Parker	1	"	s.½.	4	100	15		
807	Isaac Williams	1	"	n.½.	7	100	9	"	
808	Jacob Williams	1	"	n.½.	8	100	10	"	1
809	Edward Killiham	1	"	n.½.	9	100	10	"	1
810	Thomas Ward	1	"	n.½.	10	100	15	"	1
811	Amariah Supro	1	"	n.½.	8	100	9	"	
812	Thomas Mac Phason Chatham	1	15	s.½.	21	50	42.10	10	44

Dr. Samuel Russell's name appears at the head of the list of squatters in Raleigh Township in the 1857 Collectors Roll tax book.

To make matters worse for Russell and all of his neighbours, the government decided that they would finally offer the Raleigh Plains for sale and those who lived there would not necessarily get first chance to purchase. Opportunistic speculators — including Edwin Larwill — with questionable ethics and more political savvy, informed the commissioner of Crown Lands, who was stationed in Quebec, that the land was totally submerged and therefore not fit for agricultural purposes. Those who knew better insisted that "a large portion is as dry as the prairies of Illinois" and the rest could be drained with a lesser effort than would be required to clear the natural forest on nearby land.[5] Cutting the reeds and grasses that grew from six to nine feet high was certainly easier than cutting the elm, oak, or black ash trees that were so thick in adjoining parts of the township that children would often lose their way and vigilance committees had to be formed to rescue them.[6]

An Irish-Canadian farmer named Patrick Ryan had his eye on the lands claimed by Samuel Russell and accordingly wrote to the commissioner of Crown Lands to inquire if the lot was for sale, or if they had been legally claimed, and, if so, by whom. The reply stated that an official order-in-council signed by the attorney general had granted it to John McGregor more than half a century earlier, on July 5, 1796.[7] McGregor did not receive the original patent until May 17, 1802. The almost forgotten title was not completely cleared up until November 1859 when the late McGregor's son and heir, Duncan, took undisputed title of the property when he received the deed from the county sheriff.[8]

Having now lost any hope of getting title to land on the Raleigh Plains, the Russell family now had to squarely face an even more painful reality — the potential loss of their Chatham home. John Fleming, who had sold them the house and held the mortgage, had become exasperated that Russell was not making his payments as had been promised. Even the first payment was then two years overdue and the scheduled final payment more than two months so. Unable to collect on his own, Fleming assigned the mortgage to a man named Henry Ruttle with instructions to "hereby authorize and empower the said Henry Ruttle his heirs or assigns to collect the same in my name by any legal or equitable process or otherwise that may be necessary ..." To ensure that the transaction was legally documented, Fleming and Ruttle signed the Memorial of Assignment of Mortgage on January 11, 1858, and registered the document at the Kent Registry Office eight days later.[9] Interestingly, the value of the mortgage remained at 178 pounds, 15 shillings, which was the original purchase price.

Ruttle acted quickly and Samuel Russell had no choice but to put his mark to another document to "have assigned, transferred, set over, bargained, sold, revised, released, relinquished, and forever quit claim unto the said Henry Ruttle" any title to his home. For the sum of five shillings, a probably heartbroken Susannah surrendered any matrimonial claim and marked her X to the document that stated in part that she "hereby bars her Dower in the said Lands and relinquished the same."[10]

Chapter Fourteen

Somber Skies and Howling Tempests

We are tossed and driven on the restless sea of time;
Somber skies and howling tempests oft succeed a bright sunshine;
In that land of perfect day, when the mists are rolled away,
We will understand it better by and by.

— Charles A. Tindley, 1905

Samuel and Susannah Russell, both of whom were rapidly approaching their sixtieth year, must have felt snake-bitten, but they persevered. Despite having lost the title to their home, the family remained living among their neighbours and friends in Chatham's east end. Dr. Russell also continued to maintain his medical practice based in the Charity Building. The presence of the *Provincial Freeman* and its editor, Mary Ann Shadd Cary, in the same building ensured that life was never boring. Mrs. Shadd Cary was a remarkable woman, described by an admirer as:

> [R]ather tall, but of fine physical organization wholly feminine in appearance and demeanour has a well molded head set upon a rather slender neck, which gives her, when erect or speaking animatedly, what white folks would say, a very saucy look.... Miss Shadd's eyes are small and penetrating, and fairly flash when she is speaking. Her ideas seem to flow so fast that she, at

times, hesitates for words; yet she overcomes any appar-
ent imperfection in her speaking by the earnestness of
her manner, and the quality of her thoughts. She is a
superior woman, and it is useless to deny it.[1]

However, her fiery temper and caustic pen were guaranteed to
inspire controversy. After one of her scathing editorials in which she
attacked members of the nearby Baptist Church, the trustees (which
included her landlord) responded with an acerbic letter of their own:
"We believe Mrs. Cary to be the enemy of the Cross of Christ and when
she vilifies the names of the tried friends of the slave, we are not sur-
prised. She knows how to applaud the enemies of the Refugees ... and
to abuse their friends.[2]

We are left to wonder about the relationship that would have existed
between the mercurial editor and the doctor. Shadd Cary was deserving
of Russell's admiration as a tireless advocate for their people, an anti-
slavery warrior, and, on a more personal level, one of the teachers of the
Russell children. However, she was a vocal foe of Hiram Wilson, who
had been the family's guardian in earlier days. She was also a constant
opponent to what she referred to as "begging," or the practice of receiving charity, something of which the Russells had been among the grateful recipients. (It is interesting to note that the *Provincial Freeman* staff
cheerfully acknowledged the financial support of Lucretia Mott, who
made a generous donation to help prop up the struggling newspaper.[3])
Articles of praise for Chatham's other black physicians appeared in the
columns, but Dr. Russell was never mentioned in her newspaper other
than in the weekly advertisements for his medical practice that he placed.
Perhaps that was a good thing.

Not everyone was impressed with Russell's medical philosophy.
William Wells Brown, himself a former slave, visited Chatham in 1861
as part of a tour of several black areas of settlement in Canada. Brown
raved at the medical skill of Dr. Thomas Joiner White who, he stated,
was educated at one of the oldest universities in Maine as well as in Paris,
France. Similar kudos were bestowed upon Dr. Martin Delany, who
was highly regarded for his chosen profession and even more so for his

Image from *Autographs for Freedom*, 2nd series, page 71, edited by Julia Griffiths on behalf of the Rochester Ladies' Anti-Slavery Society. Courtesy of Kate Clifford Larson.

William Wells Brown generally had a favourable impression of Chatham as printed in The Black Abolitionist Papers: Volume II: *"Those who have ever passed down the valley of the Mississippi, or walked on the banks washed by the Potomac, will have his liveliest recollections of the appearance of the slaves revived by spending an hour in Chatham." Sadly, his impression of Dr. Samuel Russell's medical practice was less complimentary.*

reputation as a newspaper editor and lecturer. He also travelled extensively and spearheaded "the Niger Valley Exploring Expedition," which was a movement to return blacks to Africa where they could establish their own homeland. Brown described Delany as a man whose firmly held convictions and public speaking ability made him "the ablest man in Chatham, if not in America." Dr. Amos Array was deemed a bit less praiseworthy, however, grudging respect was granted because he was a reformer in the medical practice, being an "allopathist [treatment that would bring on effect different than the disease], hydropathist [natural healing powers of water], homeopathist [administering small doses of medicine that would bring on symptoms similar to that of the disease], and an eclectic [use of botanical medicine, but also conventional physiological treatments]" and possessed the unwavering faith of his patients. Although Dr. Array employed some of the same methods as Dr. Samuel Russell, Brown felt the latter to be worthy of only a passing, dismissive sneer: "I called at his gate, read his sign, my mouth beginning to feel peppery, I passed on."[4]

Samuel Russell may have learned a devastating lesson that perhaps the judgment of the naysayers concerning the practice of botanic medicine was well-founded. An epidemic of scarlet fever ravaged Chatham in 1860. The first symptom of infection was a sore throat, followed a day or two later by a rash that made the skin rough like sandpaper. High fever, sudden chills, nausea, and vomiting compounded the pain of swollen glands around the jaw and neck. Swollen tonsils and tongue, sometime coated white or dotted with yellow pustules, made swallowing extremely difficult. Flaking skin, mental confusion, and delirium accompanied severe cases.

If Dr. Russell attended a patient suffering from those debilitating symptoms, he would have held to the Thomsonian botanical treatment, and recommended a gargle of "Thomson's Pepper Sauce" composed of cayenne pepper, salt, and vinegar for the early stage. More advanced cases called for ingesting a powdered mixture of the root of the goldenseal plant, poplar bark, nervine (herbs), and cayenne pepper diluted in warm water every two or three hours. A hot onion plaster, roasted in ashes, could be applied externally to "calm the nerves of the patient."

A colleague of Russell advised that if there "were any signs of saburral embarrassment, injections of a decoction of slippery elm, or any other mucilaginous substance" was to be given. (Apparently not having a mirror, the author of this prescription ridiculed others for using extravagant wording as "unprincipled pretender, who wants to dazzle the multitude with his pedantic airs." In simpler language he accused them of being "the very root of quackery" and anyone who followed them were conceited simpletons.) These treatments, some in combination with Dr. Thomson's secret recipes, would act by relaxing the fibres of the heart and arteries and "raise a greater abundance of the essence of life."[5]

The bacteria that caused the illness easily spread to others who came into close contact. Children were especially susceptible. One newspaper named the disease the "red demon of the nursery" and commented: "We hope that it may soon depart from our midst, and leave the young buds of our affection, that are just blooming into life, to blossom and gladden our lives when we are old."[6] Susannah and Samuel were robbed of some of those buds of their affection, and, when the census taker arrived at their home in early 1861, they tearfully reported that their nineteen-year-old daughter was among those that scarlet fever had claimed within the past year. Two other children of their household also died of the disease that year — a thirteen-year-old girl and an eleven-year-old boy. Unfortunately, the census taker did not record the names of the deceased children nor identify their parents. Susannah, who would turn sixty before the year was out, was well past the normal child-bearing years so it is doubtful that she would have been the mother of the two youngest children. The Russell's eldest daughters, thirty-five-year-old Lucinda and twenty-five-year-old Catharine, both married, had returned to live in their parents' home, and, given her age, those children may have belonged to Lucinda. At any rate, grief permeated every cranny of the one-storey frame home in the way that only the death of a child can do.

At that time, the Russell family was easing apart in a variety of ways. Neither Lucinda nor Catharine's husbands were with their wives in the household and neither of them appeared in the Chatham census. Two of their siblings, sixteen-year-old William and fifteen-year-old Nancy, were still living at home — William was attending school and Nancy had found a job as a milliner, specializing in hats for women. Older brother Leonard had, like his two brothers-in-law, disappeared from the local records. Jacob, who would soon be twenty, along with his fourteen-year-old "spinster" sister Rebecca, had moved into a one-storey log cabin in nearby Harwich Township, where they cared for three young children with the surname Berry who were presumably their nieces and nephew, children of Catharine —Mary, nine; Margaret, three; and infant William.[7] This tangled living arrangement suggests that scarlet fever had forced the extended family to step in and help each other survive the best way that they could, as they always had.

Epilogue

The Last Mile of the Way

When I've gone the last mile of the way
I will rest at the close of the day;
And I know there are joys that await me,
When I have gone the last mile of the way.

— Johnson Oatman Jr., 1908

Although time must have seemed to stand still during the crisis of the beginning of the 1860s, life continued with all of its twists and turns. Jacob soon took a wife, Rosanna Jones — commonly called Annie, and the couple moved into her parents' home. They quickly filled their lives with children of their own, first Annie Maria, then Robert James, followed by Arabella.[1] Jacob was soon to learn the pain that his parents and sister had experienced when his three-week-old daughter died on August 20, 1872.[2] A year later, yet another daughter died after a three-month illness in which she wasted away, malnourished and emaciated.[3] Two years after that, his eldest, Annie, died of consumption at the tender age of eight.[4] By 1882, only Robert was left from his first children, but he was (later) joined by siblings Theodore, Alfred B., Florence, Kirby Herbert, and Jessy.[5] Jessy was only to live for ten months when on February 4, 1882, after suffering from a lung disease, she joined her sisters in death.[6] Jacob spent the remainder of his life in Chatham, living at a variety of places in Chatham's east end, working as a whitewasher, plasterer, and a common labourer.[7] His first wife, Annie, died of apoplexy on September 30, 1896, at the age of fifty-three.[8] Two years later, Jacob married a California-born widow, Clarissa Woodey.

The elusive Leonard Russell resurfaced in the 1870 census of Detroit, now married to twenty-five-year-old Elizabeth Johnson. His bride was Canadian-born, the daughter of parents from Kentucky and Virginia who had fled to the safety of the British Dominion. The couple were the proud parents of three daughters: Carlin (Catharine), seven; Louise (Elisa), six; and Ida (Idell), three. They were all listed by the census taker as having been born in Michigan. Leonard was recorded as a labourer, age twenty-nine, and unable to read or write.[9] In 1871, the family lived at 81 McComb Street before moving down the same street to 366 McComb, from which base he continued his work as a whitewasher.[10] Tragedy struck the household before the end of the decade when the young wife and mother, who had lived in the United States for thirteen years at the time, died of consumption at age thirty-five in December 1879.[11] In 1880, the now-widowed Leonard remained living in Detroit with his three daughters, along with boarder Candis Salter, who supported herself by taking in washing and ironing. Catharine, now seventeen, was in charge of keeping house, while her sisters attended school. Elisa, the middle child, was listed as the only child born in Canada, while her sisters were born in Michigan.[12]

On January 5, 1887, Leonard was awarded a contract for whitewashing and cleaning the jail in Detroit.[13] Nearing the end of that year he crossed over the Detroit River to Windsor and at age forty-seven married a widow, Josephine Lee Goodman, who was ten years his junior.[14] The couple were permanently drawn to the Canadian side of the border, and, by 1891, were living in Windsor. Their home was filled with family members — Leonard's twenty-seven-year-old daughter from his first marriage, Harriet; his son, John H., eight (by his new wife); his wife's brother Levi Lee; Lee's wife Savilla; and their infant daughter. By 1911, Leonard and Josephine had a house to themselves at 287 Howard Street where they peacefully spent their last years together until Leonard's death on August 26, 1917. The remainder of Samuel and Susannah Russell's children prove much more difficult to trace.

So many unanswered questions surround what became of the family in the latter half of the nineteenth century as their names slip away from the public records. Could it be that scarlet fever had not finished its fiendish assault in the weeks that followed the January 1861 census taker's visit to the Russells' homes? The *Chatham Weekly Planet* paid little attention to the epidemic and remained strangely silent on the subject in issue after issue. It was not until March 7, 1861, that an article mentioned: "for some time past the scarlet fever has been raging with great fatality in this town. The number of deaths that has occurred is startling — many of them taking place under circumstances that are particularly distressing." The article went on to state that one family lost four children within days and many others had lost one or two. The "most melancholy bereavement" was assigned to a family named Dolsen who had lost a daughter, then her mother within two days, and the two remaining children were gravely ill. The Russells and every other person who lost loved ones would have taken issue with the writer's insensitive assessment — however inadvertent his intent may have been — that any one family's tragedy was more profound than another's.

Even more intriguing questions are raised upon browsing the names of those who surrounded the Russell family. At the time that they squatted upon the lands of the Raleigh Plains in 1857, their nearest neighbour was a black man named Edward Brown. Living next door to Jacob and Rebecca Russell in Harwich in 1861 was a Willis and Mary Brown whose children included a daughter named Lucinda.[15] Coincidence, perhaps — after all, "Brown" is one of the most common surnames in the English language — but it tugs at the emotions to think that perhaps some of the Brown family from Maryland were eventually reunited in Canada.

Most appealing of all is the hope that perhaps Samuel and Susannah Russell eventually saw the two of their eleven children who did not accompany them to Canada after they left Maryland and ultimately made a hasty flight from the gates of a Pennsylvania prison. Did they ever meet again on one side of the border or the other? Even the question of their first names remains elusive. Given the most common of all naming patterns, is it fair to guess that one of the sons would have been named Isaac?

An investigation into the Records of the Assistant Commissioner for the District of Columbia that contain outrages against blacks in the aftermath of the Civil War reveals the account of a Calvert County incident where a white man threatened to kill a "colored" Isaac Brown because the latter had "Union sentiments." Brown was forced to flee his home looking for safety.[16] Whether or not this was the son or another relative, the story paints yet another lasting image of the pain and the uncertainty that surrounded the lives of blacks even after freedom was a legal reality. Other attacks in Calvert County, including a white man being beaten and shot at for the offence of having voted for Abraham Lincoln, a black man assaulted for not addressing a white man as "Master," and multiple charges of black children being forced into apprenticeships despite the protests of their parents, further demonstrate the uneasiness that any remaining members of the Brown family would have felt.[17]

Alexander and Olivia Somerville, Isaac Brown's former master and mistress, lost much of their fortune during the Civil War, including their

Photo by the author.

The Somerville family decided to use the traditional spelling of their surname on their memorials in the Middleham Church cemetery.

thirty-two slaves who ranged from infants to people in their mid-seventies.[18] Alexander survived the war by only a few months, dying on August 28, 1865, just days after his fifty-ninth birthday. His simple granite tombstone in the peaceful, treed cemetery of the historic Middleham Chapel has fallen off its base and offers to the family the comforting

Photo by the author.

Above: *Middleham Chapel in Calvert County, the home church for Alexander and Olivia Somerville, is located just south of their farm.*

Right: *Stained-glass window in memory of Alexander and Olivia Somerville at Middleham Chapel, Maryland.*

Photo by the author.

words "Blessed are the dead that die in the Lord." Olivia survived her husband for another nine years. Her tombstone, discoloured by time and inscribed with the most well-known passage from the twenty-third psalm, stands beside that of her husband.

The church itself, a relatively tiny brick structure constructed in the shape of a cross, rises on a slight incline and overlooks the cemetery and surrounding countryside. Already an aged building in the years that Alexander Somerville and his family attended, it is the oldest church in Calvert County, built in 1748 to replace a smaller log building that dated from 1684. The cost of the construction in the currency of the time was eighty thousand pounds of tobacco. It was for many years "a Chapel of ease" — a place of worship more conveniently located to serve those who lived at such a distance to make it difficult to attend the main parish church, which could be several miles away.[19]

The home of Alexander Somerville was within an easy wagon ride to Middleham Chapel and he and his family were respected members. Many of them are also remembered through their markers in the cemetery, but a beautiful stained glass window, which is the focal point within the sanctuary, serves as a special memorial to Alexander and his wife.

An even more striking monument belongs to Hope Hull Slatter, the former slave trader who, along with Somerville, was prominently featured in the nightmares of Isaac Brown and his family. A year and a half after shipping Brown to Louisiana, Slatter temporarily retired from his vocation, selling his slave pen in Baltimore, as well as leasing his New Orleans pen to another Baltimore trader.[20] Despite being described as "a man of much intelligence and tact, of very gentlemanly address and considerable public spirit," his occupation had made him "a sort of Pariah."[21] According to an unidentified Baltimore source who reported Slatter's death to the press and who claimed to not "entirely forget the maxim which enjoins to tread lightly o'er the ashes of the dead" the former slave trader wished to become an elite member of high society following his retirement. However, he discovered that, like the mythological garment soaked in the blood of the hydra that killed Hercules, "the shirt of Nessus was upon him and even gold was not potent enough to remove it." Despite his mansion, impressive carriages, stables of beautiful white

The tomb of Hope Hull Slatter and family in Magnolia Cemetery in Mobile, Alabama. Photo taken in 1974 by Jack E. Boucher for National Park Service Department of the Interior's Historic American Buildings Survey, Washington, D.C.

horses, and other manifestations of immense wealth, and despite his occasionally unrequited claims to be a friend of President James K. Polk, Slatter remained a social outcast.[22] He moved deeper south to Mobile, Alabama, where he purchased a grandiose building for $25,000 with the intention of turning it into a luxury hotel.[23]

It was in Mobile where he found his longed-for place in upper-class society and where his eventual death from yellow fever in the autumn of 1853 was publicly mourned. The *Picayune* of September 18 lamented the loss of "a man she can ill spare — a resident capitalist, and a liberal one too." Both his occupation and his wealth ensured his everlasting place in history and both were responsible for his magnificent tomb in Magnolia Cemetery in the city where he spent his final years.

In sharp contrast is the absence of even the crudest memorial for one of the souls on whom Alexander Somerville and Hope Hull Slatter built their fortunes. There is no stone in Maple Leaf Cemetery in Chatham, Ontario, Canada, to mark the final resting place of Samuel Russell, previously the slave Isaac Brown. No obituary appears in the *Chatham Planet* or in those many newspapers that once covered his story so passionately and extensively. No last will and testament appears in the records of the Kent County Registry Office. Likewise, those things are missing for Susannah. Perhaps it was their lifelong struggle against poverty that denied those simplest reminders of their passage. The final public recording appeared in the 1864–65 *County of Kent Gazetteer*, in a section identifying "Professionals," which listed *Samuel Russell, Chatham, doctor.* By the time that the 1871 census taker made his rounds through the east end of Chatham, neither Samuel nor Susannah was listed.

There was one more indirect record that mentioned the hero and heroine of our story, and it is most touching of all. On January 9, 1871, Sarah, one of the couple's daughters, was married. Her marriage registration recorded that she was then twenty-six, still living in Harwich Township.[24] Given her age, she would be the same daughter identified as "Nancy" in the 1861 census. Her groom, Thomas Cundle, was a widower, born in England and several years her senior. He was a farmer and former stagecoach driver. Methodist minister Alex Langford performed the ceremony. Permelia Langford, the reverend's wife, and Solomon Merrill, a Chatham hotel keeper whose tavern would bear his name for a century more, served as witnesses. The bride was only a child when she and her family first came to Canada, when they left their surname behind and became the Russells. But today, on the most special day of her life, unlike her siblings when they were in a similar circumstance, she used her birth name. When asked for the name of her parents, Reverend Langford entered the reply into the register:[25]

Acknowlegements, Notes on Sources, and the Case of The Two Isaac Browns

My interest in Isaac Brown was first kindled in January 1977. As did millions of others, I sat in front of a television set for eight consecutive nights, mesmerized by the dramatization of Alex Haley's book *Roots*. Although fascinated with history from an early age, and despite growing up in Buxton, which was once a haven for fugitive slaves and was then (as now) a place that had a museum that celebrated the stories of those remarkable people, I had never taken the time to find out about my own ancestors. Watching that miniseries irrevocably changed that.

The first steps were to grill parents, grandfather, great aunts, and more distant cousins. Sadly, they knew but little of our family history in the days before emancipation, a fact that I came to learn was not uncommon among people of African descent. Visits to both nearby and more distant museums, libraries, and historians gradually revealed tiny bits of the fragmented recorded individual stories. The generous-hearted members of the Kent Branch Genealogical Society, particularly Helen Blackburn, Wendy Barry, and Joan Griffin, although strangers to me at the time, were helpful beyond belief in supplying information and guiding me to the records that might reveal some small detail that would add some "flesh to the bones" of long-deceased relatives.

I first learned of my great-great-great-grandfather, Isaac Brown, thanks to the late Arlie Robbins's pioneering research on early enslaved families who fled to Canada in the mid-nineteenth century. Arlie's voluminous notes and family trees, deposited in the museum that she helped found in 1967 (then known as The Raleigh Township

Centennial Museum now rechristened The Buxton National Historic Site & Museum) included mention of Isaac Brown and his family, all of whom were among the earliest residents of The Elgin Settlement and Buxton Mission, Canada's largest planned settlement for fugitive slaves.

Months of research added pieces to the puzzle that was Isaac Brown. The search for early tangible details on all of the family members was difficult since the 1851 census for Raleigh Township is lost. Thankfully, the Chatham Kent Registry Office has microfilmed copies of the land transactions, which revealed that on September 3, 1851, Isaac Brown, "yeoman," bought one acre on the military road that was at the very heart Buxton, comprised of the northern half of Lot 9, Concession 12 in Raleigh Township. He paid Joshua and Elizabeth Shepley "two hundred pounds of lawful money of Canada." The deed contains a heart-wrenching clause. Although the Shepleys were willing to sell their farm, they could not bear to lose title to a tiny sacred portion, and included the phrase: "excepting a small part of the said half lot containing the graves of three children of said grantor and extending one foot each way beyond the said graves."

The annual tax records, now housed at the Buxton Museum, thanks to the generous donation of the late Clarence and Cookie Pratt, reveal ever-evolving personal and property information. In 1852, Isaac Brown is listed as fifty-six years old. In addition to his land, he owned two horses worth $20.00 and two cows worth $4.00. By the next year he has acquired an additional fifty acres, across the road from his original purchase.

According to a printed copy of the proceedings, which are held in Cornell University's amazing Samuel J. May Anti-Slavery Collection (much of which is available online), Isaac represented Buxton at a "General Convention for the Improvement of the Colored Inhabitants of Canada" held at the First Baptist Church in Amherstburg on June 16 and 17, 1853. The list of delegates was a who's who of black community leaders from Amherstburg, Anderdon, Buxton, Colchester, Dresden, and Chatham, all in the southern part of Canada West; as well as from Detroit, Michigan, Madison, Indiana, and from Cleveland, Oberlin, and Urbana, Ohio, in the United States.

Isaac's status is confirmed by his appointment by his peers to be a member of the Business Committee. After thoughtful deliberation, this committee made recommendations on the subjects of emigration, agriculture, temperance, education, statistics, finances, and a constitution for a Provincial League. The members vilified the United States government for its inhumanity, but praised Queen Victoria and Canada for offering an asylum, and vowed to defend the country whenever called upon. They thanked Harriet Beecher Stowe for her monumental work *Uncle Tom's Cabin*, which exposed slavery in a light not previously shown. Showing that they had not forgotten their own past, they agreed to offer a letter of support for a fundraising effort to purchase and free the sister of a Canadian minister who was to be sold from Virginia to the Deep South. They also denounced the system of "begging" that brought shame to the former slaves who wanted to remove any question as to their ambition and independence. Isaac Brown was one of five men appointed to an executive committee to ensure that the recommendations of the conference were carried out and that arrangements be made for a like meeting the following year. These men were also charged with the daunting task "to supervise the general interest of the colored people of Canada."

By 1854 the Raleigh tax assessor noted that Isaac had two dogs — one of those small details that helps paint a picture of a familial scene. The total property was valued at $325, and, based on that, Isaac was assessed to perform seven days' statute labour, which was the obligation of each male citizen to perform public work, such as building roads or drainage ditches. According to Raleigh Township published records held by the Buxton Museum, as well as some in my personal collection, on January 29, 1855, the Township Council recognized Isaac for the respect he had earned when they appointed him "Fence Viewer," to settle property line disputes, oversee proper dimensions of fences, and other such responsibilities. This was an extremely important position at the time as farms were being surveyed out of virgin forest and lot lines were inexactly delineated by an axe's notch on a tree.

That same year, Isaac and his wife Mary Jane, along with the founder of the Buxton Settlement and their neighbour Reverend William King and his wife Jemima, each mortgaged one of their farms by jointly borrowing four hundred pounds from the Commercial Building and Investment Society of Toronto. On that document, Isaac signed his name rather than making his mark with an X as he had done on his original deed. Also interesting from a human standpoint, the farm that Isaac and Mary Jane mortgaged was now one hundred acres minus an area containing *six* graves. Perhaps Isaac himself was soon to enlarge that area. The year 1855 is the final time that he, at age fifty-eight, was listed in the tax records. Beginning in 1856, his home farm is listed under his widow Mary Jane Brown and his second farm under his son-in-law Edward Prince, who had married the Browns' daughter, Eliza.

In the Chatham Public Library's microfilmed copy of the 1861 personal census, only grandfather Brown's widow and some of his children appear. Mary Jane Brown, fifty-three years of age, born in the United States, was the head of the household. Her unmarried children still lived with her — Elizabeth, twenty-five and William, twenty, both born in the United States. Their ten-year-old brother, John, was the only one born in Canada West. Also living with them were Peter and Sarah King, twenty-one and twenty, respectively. They were two of the sources of inspiration for Reverend William King to seek out a place in Canada where he could free them, along with their mother and the twelve other slaves that he had either bought or inherited while he lived in Louisiana.

The agricultural census for that year shed further light on what the Brown family's lives were like in the short time since Isaac's death. On their home farm they had twenty-one of their one hundred acres under cultivation, fourteen acres under crop, six acres of pasture, and one acre of orchard or garden. Seventy-three acres were still virgin forest. Their land had appreciated considerably and was then valued at $1,410, with an additional $59 worth of farm implements needed to grow their crops of spring wheat, rye, oats, buckwheat, Indian corn, potatoes, turnips, beans, and hay. They now had five cows for beef, three for breeding and for milk, five horses, and eleven pigs.

At that time, daughter Eliza Brown Prince, her husband, three children, and a ten-year-old boy whom the family had taken in, lived beside her husband's mother, a few miles to the northeast of her parent's home and just outside of the settlement proper. The Princes would have three more children within the next five years. Tragically, Eliza died in March 1866. All six of her children were under the age of ten. While mourning her daughter, Mary Jane Brown did what grandparents have done throughout history and did what she could to care for her grandchildren.

She and two of her sons joined with her widowed son-in-law, Edward Prince, to take legal action against two unscrupulous men who attempted to take the farm that Isaac Brown had once purchased and that became his daughter Eliza's inheritance after his death. Chatham lawyer John Van Raay was kind enough to take me to the lawyer's communal private law library in that city to research that case. Trips to the Archives of Ontario to examine the papers of the presiding judge and to University of Windsor's Law Library provided more. Before their untimely deaths, both Isaac Brown and his daughter had made the mistake of not properly registering the purchase at the county registry office. It would be three years before the minor Prince children were finally awarded title to their grandfather's and mother's farm.

The aging grandmother Brown went even further to express her love by taking two of her grandchildren — the eldest and the youngest — into her home. The youngest grandchild, Alpheus, would eventually be my great-great uncle. It was he who, as an elderly man, left a further clue about Isaac Brown. In an interview with a reporter from *The Windsor Daily Star* that appeared in the January 15, 1938, edition, he stated that Isaac was a runaway slave who had escaped into a northern state. Although Isaac had died before Alpheus was born, the latter was able to draw on stories that his grandmother had told him when he was a boy. That newspaper, which I found in the archives of the *Windsor Star*, further fuelled my fascination with this distant ancestor. What was the story behind his enslavement and his escape? Who helped him, if anyone? How and when did he meet his wife? Was she also a slave and were their children? What were the details of his flight to Canada? Could I find out more about their lives in Buxton, on a farm just down the road from my home?

Other details came to light after years of further research. As would be expected, the Brown family attended St. Andrew's Presbyterian Church immediately opposite their home that was superintended by Reverend King. The late Mrs. Kathleen King kindly loaned me the records of the church to confirm that fact. The school and post office were also directly across the road from them, as was the beautiful bronze bell that was donated in

November 1850 by the coloured inhabitants of Pittsburgh, who wished to support the bold experiment at Buxton. The Browns lived at the enviable proximity to hear it ring, as tradition has it, whenever a new family successfully arrived from the land of slavery to the Queen's dominions.

I followed the lives of Mary Jane Brown and all of her children, looking at census, church, property, marriage, birth, baptism, and death records in municipal, provincial, and federal archives. Searches in diaries and the many newspaper articles that carried contemporary stories of Buxton were rarely fruitful for finding specific information on this particular family, but always interesting in general. Letters from neighbours and friends James and John Rapier, which are held in the Moorland Spingarn Archives at Howard University in Washington, D.C., respectfully, mention both Mary Jane Brown and her daughter Eliza.

Many days of wading through American census in the archives of the Allen County Public Library's Genealogy Center in Fort Wayne, Indiana, the National Archives in Washington, and several other repositories were disappointing when I could not find the Brown family prior to their coming to Canada. What I did discover was that Isaac Brown's children and grandchildren occasionally — but not always — gave their parent's or grandparent's place of birth as Maryland. When Mary Jane Brown died on September 30, 1883, after suffering from a stroke that left her paralyzed for two weeks, her youngest son, who was the informant for the death certificate, stated that his mother was seventy-eight years old and born in Maryland.

Mention of that particular state raised an exciting possibility when, while looking for something else several years later, I accidentally stumbled across a reference to a document entitled "Case of the Slave Isaac Brown, An Outrage Exposed," which focused on a slave from Maryland. As any genealogist or historian has experienced, the mere thought that this could possibly be an ancestor was thrilling! Now I had to somehow find a copy of this elusive pamphlet. That was soon achieved after discovering that the Library of Congress had digitized it and made it available on their American Memory website under the heading "Slaves and the Courts, 1740–1860." While the pamphlet gave a fascinating overview, of course, there was much more to learn.

Luckily at that time (January 2003), I belonged to an international group of Underground Railroad researchers that had been brought together by Denver, Colorado, author Jacqueline Tobin for the purpose of collaborating on the subject. I immediately emailed the list asking for help in locating the pamphlet. The always reliable and eminently knowledgeable Christopher Densmore, curator at the Friends Historical Library at Swarthmore College in Pennsylvania, replied with a few more details, offering to find a copy of the original and send it to me. He also mentioned that the *Pennsylvania Freeman* had covered the case.

Reinforcing the notion that it is always a good idea to keep good notes when researching and that it is important to occasionally go through long-forgotten files, I retraced some steps at the Robarts Library at the University of Toronto. There, they house two rolls of microfilm that contain the correspondence of the American Missionary Association and the missionaries and teachers in Canada who are under their auspices. Sure enough, there was a letter from Reverend Hiram Wilson, dated in London, Canada West, on August 6, 1847, announcing: "You will rejoice to learn that Isaac Brown (alias Saml Rufsell) with his numerous & interesting family of a wife & 9 children from the house of bondage reached Dawn on the 28th ult. in good health & spirits." Now I finally knew where the family landed when they came to Canada. Thus began a reinvigorated search for what became of them. How I wished that Hiram Wilson had mentioned them again in his voluminous correspondence and that he would have given the first names of the wife and nine children. But sadly, that was not the case. But at least I knew the name of their husband and father. Reasoning in my own mind that since he had been caught and imprisoned in Philadelphia while using this name, "Samuel Russell" was now a useless alias, particularly since he was now free and safe in Canada, and he would revert to his true identity as "Isaac Brown." But still, researching anyone with the surname "Brown" was only slightly less challenging (and occasionally overwhelming) than looking for a "Smith" or "Jones."

Even though I had previously conducted endless research on Isaac Brown, I started at the beginning again, looking for clues that may have been missed previously. Naturally, the logical place to begin was with the Dawn Settlement, the only concrete mention of his location. But

I could find no further mention of him — not in the 1851 census, not in the records of the Western District that are held in the Archives of Ontario, not in local newspapers held at the Dresden or Chatham public libraries, not in the Anglican Church Archives of the Diocese of Huron at University of Western Ontario, not in the land records of the Kent County Registry Office, the Chatham-Kent Archives, or in the University of Windsor Archives in the Leddy Library, which holds some early Kent County records. Even the usual techniques of strolling through pioneer cemeteries or browsing marriage, birth, and death records at the provincial archives or Kent Branch Genealogical Society's collection held no firm evidence. Of course, while using these same sources, I was always watching for "my" Isaac Brown who lived in Buxton, also in the County of Kent. After all, he too was a middle-aged runaway slave with several children who could be identified and had a documented Maryland connection.

Not having much luck in Kent, I repeated the same procedures in other parts of the province, particularly in the Queen's Bush area where Reverend Samuel Young died and was buried, and where Hiram Wilson seemed to leave a veiled hint about the identity of one man in particular who was inconsolable at Young's funeral. The Wellington County Museum has a good collection of genealogical information on pioneers of that area. The Ontario Genealogical Society has their province-wide holdings in the Gladys Allison Canadiana Room at the North York Central Branch of the Toronto Public Library. These include transcriptions of tombstones throughout Ontario. Among the things I hoped to find there was evidence of a monument for the guardian angel, Reverend Young, but it was not to be. Nor was there one for Isaac or Susannah.

The pamphlet on the Pennsylvania court case of the slave Isaac Brown opened up vast possibilities for research on the American side of the border. Old friends, whom my wife Shannon, who is curator of the Buxton National Historic Site & Museum, and I have been fortunate to meet over the years, gladly offered their expertise and suggestions. Foremost among them was Charles Brewer, a superb historian who lives in Washington, D.C., the home of archival gold mines. As he always does, Charles jumped in with both feet and examined many records on my behalf over a period of years. He is imaginative in thinking of what to look for, well-connected with other historians and repositories, and familiar with records that most people would not even think of pursuing. Generous and humble, he deserves my sincerest gratitude for the many things that he contributed to this as well as to my previous book.

Dennis Gannon, another historian, who could be described with much the same words, is the premier authority on Hiram Wilson and extremely knowledgeable on the broader subject of black history. Dennis graciously shared volumes of his own research, allowing me to get to know the missionary who guided the Brown family into Canada and offered them their first home in freedom.

Thankfully, the Isaac Brown story had grabbed headlines in many newspapers across North America. I would like to recognize some of the repositories that hold microfilmed copies of some of these that I used in researching this story: The Leddy Library at University of Windsor; Purdy/Kresge Library, Wayne State University, Detroit; Library of Congress, Washington, D.C; Central Branch of the Free Library of Philadelphia; Maryland State Archives; Friends Historical Library at Swarthmore College, Pennsylvania; and Weldon Library at University of Western Ontario, London. As time has gone on, more newspapers have been digitized and are available online by subscription: Accessible Archives and other historical newspaper collections through Godfrey Memorial Library, Genealogy Bank, and *New Orleans Times-Picayune. OurOntario.ca* Community Newspapers Collection has the two major black Canadian newspapers —*Voice of the Fugitive* and *Provincial Freeman* — online for free.

In early 2005, I decided to contact the Calvert County (Maryland) Historical Society to ask if they knew anything more on either Isaac Brown or Alexander Somerville. Archivist Karen Sykes quickly responded that she was not aware of the case but, intrigued by the story, forwarded my email to Kirsti Uunila, historic preservation planner at the Calvert County Department of Planning and Zoning. Kirsti, in turn, contacted Ms. Pat Melville, archivist for the Maryland State Archives, also known as The Hall of Records. All were excited by the story and Pat decided to further research the saga by using the collections at her disposal. In addition to her position as archivist, Pat was also editor of the archive's interdepartmental newsletter, *The Archivist's Bulldog*. In that role, she wrote and published an article, *Slave Isaac Brown: A Case of Legal Maneuvering* in honour of Black History Month. She credited Millington Longwood, a staff member from the Maryland Underground Railroad Project, with assisting in the research. I would like to thank both Pat and Millington for their work and for uncovering and sending me some new details that I had not seen. I also appreciate the assistance of several other staff at the Maryland State Archives, including Chris Haley, on our numerous trips to their facility. Calvert County's Karen Sykes and Kirsti Uunila deserve special mention for their interest, encouragement, and help over a period that extended well beyond our initial contact. The County Courthouse had been destroyed by fire in 1882, so any records that they may have held about Isaac Brown or Alexander Somerville were lost. Therefore, the help of these historians who are working to uncover this history from the ashes is invaluable.

The next exciting development came quickly thereafter. Our friend Tony Burroughs, who is probably the most well-known and qualified genealogist specializing in African-American research, contacted me and suggested that I submit a request to a new Canadian television series called *Ancestors in the Attic*, asking them to focus one of their programs on an interesting case of an enslaved ancestor who fled to freedom. I took him up on that advice, hoping to find out once and for all if the two Isaac Browns were indeed the same person, and soon heard back from Chris Robinson, one of the producers. They assigned the Isaac Brown story as "Case #162" and were eager to pursue it. I supplied all of the information — by then a hefty amount — that I had accumulated to that point. By March 2006, *Ancestors* had hired genealogists in Pennsylvania and Ottawa, and Chris and I were in constant contact. Stephanie Hoover did some of the work in Pennsylvania and Patricia Kennedy conducted extensive investigation at Library and Archives Canada on the Executive Council and Lord Elgin's records, as well as the civil secretary's correspondence. Related to Patricia's search are the Records of the Governor General's Office, also known as Despatches to and from the Colonial Office (RG7-G-1, microfilm C160) and the papers of James Bruce, Earl of Elgin, then governor general of Canada, which are published in *Elgin-Grey Papers, 1846–1852* by J.O. Patenaude, Ottawa, 1937, both of which I was able to access at the Weldon Library at the University of Western Ontario.

Arrangements were made for the director and crew to come to Buxton on June 6, 2005, and film the episode with the museum as the backdrop. On June 5, I was dying to know what hidden gems they were going to spring on me the next day. It was then that I received a call, apologizing that they were unable to find any other substantial details beyond what I or Charles Brewer had already uncovered. There would be no "Aha!" moment to commit to film so the shoot was cancelled at the eleventh hour. Oh well, it was an interesting experience. Keep on digging.

One great thing happened as an indirect result of the investigation by the historians who had been engaged by the television producers, however inadvertent it may have been. Jenny Masur, a friend we had met periodically over the years who is the National Capital Region coordinator for the National Parks Service Underground Railroad Network to Freedom, learned of the search for Isaac Brown and my connection to it. She contacted Karen James, coordinator for Underground Railroad History for the Pennsylvania Bureau of Archives and History, who was doing work with Philadelphia court records. The timing was perfect. Karen had discovered a series of rich documents housed at the Pennsylvania State Archives, indexed under RG-26 Extradition Files, in the Papers of the Governors. Among those records were arrest warrants for Isaac Brown from both Pennsylvania and Maryland, testimony from the slave traders who tried to assist in returning Brown to Maryland, letters from Brown's Quaker lawyers and supporters and — most importantly — the testimony of Isaac Brown's wife and daughter! Finally, I would be able to identify them. Although I had never met this thoughtful and wonderful person who contacted me out of the blue, I seem to recall developing an instant crush on Karen James, but don't tell my wife.

When Karen's package arrived in the mail on May 24, 2006, it felt like Christmas morning. The copies of the original documents were rich with more information. In a way that typescript can never do, the handwritten letters gave a more intimate feel for the terror experienced by Isaac Brown and his family and for the passionate support given to them by others. I felt the indignation of the Calvert County Grand Jury as they passed sentence on the fugitive slave who was then held in a Philadelphia jail, the cool official detachment of Governor Pratt as he requested that Brown be extradited back to Maryland, the pain in the testimony of daughter Lucinda as she relived her time that she and her father spent in the Prince Frederick Jail, and the injustice of it all that had descended on wife Susannah.

As suggested above, the most exciting detail was the identification of the daughter as "Lucinda Brown" and the wife as "Susanna [*sic*] Brown." It was a minor disappointment that the wife's name was not "Mary Jane," the name of my great-great-great grandmother, as I had expected it to be. But by then I was so captivated by the family and their story that it seemed relatively unimportant. At least now I could return to my research in Canada West in search of a Lucinda (or any variations like Lucy or Cindy) Brown and Susanna (or variations Susannah, Sue, Susan, Hannah or Anna) Brown. Many more months of searching for them proved futile. The thought crept into my mind that, as researchers find over and over again, the same people appear in different documents with different first names, usually explained by having an official first name at birth, but being commonly called by a middle name or names. Just one example is found in Karolyn Smardz Frost's award-winning book *I've Got A Home In Glory Land* in which the heroine is called "Ruthie" in early documents, but is "Lucie" after she came north, eventually into Canada. In the absence of finding any record of a "Susannah Brown," there was still a faint possibility that she was the same person as "Mary Jane Brown" from Maryland and married to Isaac Brown.

After seemingly exhausting the Canadian sources, I returned my focus to the United States. One evening in early 2010, while passing time at the Purdy/Kresge Library at Wayne State University, trying to kill an hour or two before a Civil War television documentary screening, I casually browsed through a microfilm of a New York City abolitionist newspaper, *The National Anti-Slavery Standard*, when I had one of those few and far between "Eureka!" moments. The September 30, 1847, edition carried a remarkably lengthy and detailed account of Isaac Brown and family's flight to Canada in company with Reverend Samuel Young, who provided the first-hand information. He mentioned the complete route that they had taken, the people who helped, and those who interfered. He supplied personal details such as Susannah's illness in Buffalo, which he described as "the mother was broken down," and their additional three-day delay in Detroit as they tried to find a boat to take them to Lake St. Clair. And there were touching scenes of a stranger in Rochester who, upon hearing Brown's story, offered to donate a wood stove to warm his family once they reached their final destination. Those images made me want to travel much of the same route and see some of the things that they might have seen. So off we went days later, with Shannon, who was always a tremendous help and supporter in preparing this book, being the other half of "we."

We drove through Buffalo and Rochester to observe and absorb that part of the route. Our first stop was Syracuse, New York, for a visit to the Special Collections Research Center at Syracuse University Library to re-examine The Gerrit Smith Papers and to look for additional information on Reverend Luther Lee, whom the Browns met along the way. We next went to the abolitionist hotbed of Boston, where the family began their westward journey to Canada. Two extraordinary scholars and special people were connected with this leg of our trip. Kate Clifford Larson, professor in the Department of History at Simmons College and author of *Bound for the Promised Land: Harriet Tubman, Portrait of an American Hero*, not only supplied tips for our research, but met us, guided us through Boston's historic districts, and welcomed us into her home. Kate also introduced me to Kathryn Grover, historian and author from New Bedford, Massachusetts. Like Kate, Kathryn has an extensive range of interests and expertise and is one of those generous souls who share both. Many of our Boston and later New York City stops were based on Kathryn's recommendations, and we were not disappointed.

The Massachusetts Historical Society (MHS) is appropriately housed in an elegant old New England building. There, we looked through papers of individuals who were involved in the Isaac Brown case, including the William Lloyd Garrison Papers and those of Edmund Quincy, which are in the Quincy, Wendell, Holmes and Upham Family Papers, as well as those of some of their contemporary abolitionist friends who could have been involved, such as the Theodore Parker Papers and Samuel May Papers. Letters of Francis Jackson are also scattered in some of the collections. Records of the Underground Railroad organization, the Boston Anti-Man-Hunting League, were interesting to look at, but did not mention Isaac Brown. The papers of Amos A. Lawrence provided some insight on his assistance to the Dawn Settlement and his support and correspondence with Hiram Wilson's co-worker, Josiah Henson. The MHS also has an extensive collection of photographs of American abolitionists, many of which they have placed online and some of whom appear in this book.

The Houghton Library at Harvard University houses The American Freedmen's Inquiry Commission Records and those of one of its commissioners, Samuel Gridley Howe, in the Howe Family Papers. Howe visited Chatham (as well as other black centres in Canada West) in 1863 and interviewed many of its residents. Unfortunately, the name Isaac Brown/Samuel Russell did not appear in either of those collections. However, in the microfilm collection of the Lamont Library next door to Houghton, those interviews do appear as part of War Department, Letters Received by the Adjutant General. Luckily, a black man from Toronto named Thomas Smallwood was interviewed, and he recalled some intimate details of the Brown case, including the fact that Isaac Brown was arrested in Philadelphia after having sent a letter to his grown-up son who remained in Maryland. Smallwood's words suggested that he had met with Samuel Young when the minister was on his way to Montreal to meet with Lord Elgin. The original papers are housed at the National Archives, Washington, D.C., as a part of Record Group 94.

The Boston Public Library has an incredible anti-slavery collection that is card-indexed by correspondent and by place. While there we looked at a wide variety of materials, but far too often became sidetracked from the original goal. However, I focused long enough to read the appropriate date range when Isaac Brown would have been in Boston in the diary of Edmund Quincy that spanned 1824–50, and read letters from Francis Jackson, Samuel May, Sydney Howard Gay, and Edmund Quincy. The microfilmed *Anti-Slavery Collection, 18th–19th Centuries*, originally from the Library of the Society of Friends, is a huge and interesting set of documents.

From Boston we travelled to the Rare Book & Manuscript Library within the Butler Library at Columbia University in New York City. The staff person who dealt with us was an absolute delight. As Kathryn Grover had suggested, The Sydney Howard Gay Papers were an amazing collection. Gay was the editor of *The National Anti-Slavery Standard*, and, as mentioned previously, knew intimate details of Isaac Brown's case. Unfortunately, Gay has been an almost forgotten figure in the anti-slavery movement, but even a perfunctory look at his papers proves that he is worthy of much more acclaim. That will inevitably come when some scholar reveals the contents of this collection to the historical community, thus bringing Gay into the company of revered figures such as William Still, Thomas Garrett, Levi Coffin, and others of that ilk.

After a brief stop in Connecticut at Yale University's Gilder Lehrman Center for the Study of Slavery, Resistance, and Abolition, we continued on to Philadelphia. The Historical Society of Pennsylvania has the huge collection, The Papers of the Pennsylvania Abolition Society: 1775–1975, where we found many nuggets related to the Brown case and the lawyers who assisted him. Photos of Moyamensing Prison and records of The Philadelphia Society for Alleviating the Miseries of Public Prisons were also illuminating to get a feel for the experiences of the prisoners. The Central Branch of the Free Library of Philadelphia holds microfilmed copies of most of the city newspapers, which were a rich source of information. The newspapers we scoured there were: *Commercial List & Philadelphia Price Current*, *Germantown Telegraph*, *North American & U.S. Gazette*, *Pennsylvania Freeman*, *Pennsylvanian Weekly*, *Philadelphia Bulletin*, *Philly Inquirer*, and *U.S. Gazette*.

One of the most pleasurable stops was to the offices of the United States National Parks Service. After meeting and sharing the Isaac Brown story with Coxey Toogood, historian of Interpretation and Visitors Services at Independence National Historical Park, and Rick Starr, education program developer, we were treated to a personalized, behind-the-scenes tour of Independence Hall and Congress Hall where the court hearings took place. It was gripping to picture the manacled prisoner hopelessly cowering before the judges who looked down on him from their lofty bench. Special also was a visit to Mother Bethel African

Methodist Episcopal Church, just minutes away on foot from 172 Pine, the narrow street where Isaac Brown lived and was first arrested. The Browns may very well have attended this historic church and at the very least would have known many of its members.

Just a few miles outside of Philadelphia is Swarthmore College, and on the campus grounds with all of its Old World charm is The Friends Historical Library. The presence of Lucretia Mott, one of the college's founders, is still palpable there, most dramatically manifested with a marble bust. Within the Special Collections Department, Christopher Densmore guided us through their collection of the Mott Manuscripts, 1831–1959 and the Abby Hopper Gibbons Papers. Swarthmore has also joined with two other Quaker colleges, Haverford and Bryn Mawr, to digitize records under the title "Quakers & Slavery" and make them freely accessible to everyone at *http://trilogy.brynmawr.edu/speccoll/quakersandslavery*. Among those records are the letters of Isaac Tatum Hopper, who, along with other family members, was involved in the Brown rescue.

Next on our itinerary was the H. Furlong Baldwin Library of The Maryland Historical Society in Baltimore to study the 1832 Census for Free People of Color that was contained in a much larger collection Maryland State Colonization Society Papers, 1827–1871. Knowing that Susannah Brown, as well as any children born to her at that time would have been free, I hoped to be able to locate her and thereby find the names of more of her children. Unfortunately, neither her name nor Lucinda's appeared in the list for Calvert County. However, there was a Mary Brown who, judging by other research evidence, lived in the immediate vicinity of Alexander Somerville. Henry Harrison, the sheriff of the county who took the census, recorded Mary as twenty-five years old, just the right age to be my ancestor, Mary Jane Brown. Perhaps ...

The Colonization Papers also include registers of manumissions and lists where owners have agreed to free their slaves upon their reaching a certain age. Separated by county, the names of the slaves are registered beside that of their owner. Many hours were spent both in Baltimore and at Wayne State University going through those thirty-one rolls of microfilm trying to find a "Susannah" in Calvert County who may have had her freedom registered, and also for a registration by Alexander Somerville, which would confirm the promise that was widely reported that he would free Isaac Brown upon reaching the age of thirty-five. If that could be found, it might include the name of Isaac's unfortunate brother whom Somerville had killed while enraged at his slave for having returned too late from his wedding. Unfortunately, those particular records do not appear in this collection. My thanks go to assistant librarian Jennifer Copeland for her help with these records and to Jerry M. Hynson for publishing *Free African Americans of Maryland 1832* (Willow Bend Books, Winchester, Maryland, 2000), which first made me aware of this census.

After leaving Baltimore, we went to Washington, D.C., where we visited the Manuscript Reading Room in the Madison Building of the Library of Congress to check the American Missionary Association Papers for correspondence of those abolitionists, including Hiram Wilson, who had a relationship with Isaac Brown. Knowing how closely knit the anti-slavery community was, we explored the papers of other possible confidantes such as Lewis Tappan, George Whipple, and William Harned. (The Robarts Library in Toronto has the two microfilmed reels of Canadian correspondence only, but the Library of Congress, as well as the University of Maryland Library and perhaps a few other institutions, has the complete collection of 261 reels. The originals are housed at Amistad Research Center at Tulane University, New Orleans.) The Lewis Tappan Papers are also held in the former, and several other repositories, including The Dana Porter Library at the University of Waterloo (Ontario), hold microfilmed copies. Thanks also to the staff at the newspaper room in the Library of Congress for checking for and retrieving some of the "penny newspapers" that were held off-site, such as *Cummings' Evening Telegraphic Bulletin* and *Spirit of the Times and Daily Keystone*, the latter of which extensively covered the Brown legal case in Philadelphia.

Next, with Charles Brewer on board, we travelled to Calvert County to see the land where Isaac Brown and family once lived. Alexander Somerville's plantations are now within the fenced-off grounds of the Calvert Cliffs Nuclear Power Plant. Unfortunately, since the tragedy of 9/11, the public is no longer allowed within the gates. However, we did get to see the countryside and feel some of its memories. It was particularly moving to walk through the bucolic cemetery where Alexander

Somerville, his wife, and family members are buried. As luck would have it, an elderly couple who are parishioners at the Middleham Chapel arrived about the same time and kindly invited us in while they tidied the church for Sunday's service. Their justifiable pride in their historic church was warming and I hope that they will forgive me for having forgotten their names so I could properly thank them here. The imposing stained glass that bears the names of Alexander and Cornelia Olivia Somerville is truly impressive. Funny how seeing that window and looking at their tombstones in that beautiful setting diminished any ill feelings that I might have unconsciously harboured for the man who caused so much pain to the family I had came to love. The combination of looking at those symbols of remembrance and their reminders of the passage of time put things into a different perspective and dispersed a peaceful melancholy.

Detroit was the final United States leg of the Browns' flight before entering Canada. My admiration goes to John Palacsek, curator of Marine History at Dossein Great Lakes Museum on Belle Isle in Detroit, for immediately recognizing the names of both the captain and the ship that carried the family across Lake Erie, and my thanks to him for sharing his knowledge of Captain Shepherd's abolitionist activities. A better understanding of the Michigan anti-slavery movement and of Charles H. Stewart is provided by the good folks at Ann Arbor District Library who have digitized the *Signal of Liberty* newspaper and made it freely available at *http://signalofliberty.aadl.org*. It was somewhat disappointing that there was no mention of Brown's passage through Detroit in published reports or interviews done with members of the Colored Vigilance Committee, including William Lambert (*Detroit Tribune*, January 17, 1887) and George de Baptiste (*Detroit Post*, May 14, 1870).

Distance and a shortage of time (and money) prevented travelling to some of the places I would have like to have gone, so I would like to express my gratitude to the people who examined their collections and responded to my queries. Judy Bolton, the head of public services of the Special Collections at Louisiana State University Library in Baton Rouge, checked the Kenner Family Papers for mention of Isaac Brown during the short time that he was in the New Orleans area and briefly belonged to William Butler Kenner. Matthew Turi, manuscripts reference librarian at the Southern Historical Collection at Wilson Library of the University of North Carolina at Chapel Hill, looked through the Francis Rawn Shunk Papers to see if the governor of Pennsylvania had mentioned Brown in private correspondence. Dennis Gannon, Marie Carter, Karolyn Smardz Frost, and Blair Newby generously shared letters from The Hiram Wilson Papers housed in Ohio's Oberlin College Library Archives. A historian at Historic New England, Quincy House, in Quincy, Massachusetts, also shared some of her knowledge of one-time resident, Josiah Quincy, who provided the train ticket to the Browns and Reverend Young as they departed from the east.

One of my deepest regrets and sincerest appreciation goes to Charlene Mires, associate professor of history at Villanova University in Pennsylvania. Charlene's graduate students worked on a project about court cases at Philadelphia's Independence Hall and adjacent Congress Hall. Their collected work was published internally as *In Pursuit of Liberty: African American Court and Prison Stories from Philadelphia, 1820's–1840's.* One of the students, Kristi Johnston, wrote an article on Isaac Brown. I applaud Charlene and all of her students for their investigative work and thank them for helping me better understand the Philadelphia court system. I express my regret that time and uncertainty of schedule did not allow me to accept their thoughtful invitation to meet with them and have an event that celebrated Isaac Brown. I would like to also extend a second word of thanks to Coxey Toogood, who assisted in initiating the project at Villanova and who kindly invited me to share the Brown story at a training session for her interpretive staff. We hope that we can arrange this sometime in the near future.

After returning from our trip and completing the story with the new information we had gathered, there remained an overwhelming, disturbing thought — what became of this family after they arrived in Canada? It was tempting to conclude that, in all likelihood, this must be the same Isaac Brown as my ancestor. But conjecture is never good enough. I decided to use *Ancestry.com* one more time to try to track this family down, only this time doing a search from 1850 to 1881 (without using a surname) in both Canada and the United States for any and all families that had both a "Lucinda" and a "Susannah."

Acknowlegements, Notes on Sources, and the
Case of the Two Isaac Bowns

Voila! In the 1861 census for Chatham, there was indeed both a daughter "Lucinda" and mother "Susannah" living in the same household. And, as you already know from reading this book, the head of the household was "Samuel Russell"— the same name that Isaac Brown had adopted when he first fled from slavery. So many months wasted and the name was before me all of the time. The emotion that I experienced was relief, mixed with a teaspoon of joy, and cup full of embarrassment that it took so long to find this answer. Perhaps that error in judgment can be partially explained and forgiven because, as we will soon see, the father was called Isaac Brown in one more official Ontario document. At any rate, this new information required retracing many steps, now researching the surname "Russell." New leads included examining the Mary Ann Shadd Cary Papers held privately and generously shared by Edward and Maxine Robbins.

Over the course of researching this story, there were many archivists, librarians, historians, and others who listened, made suggestions, or helped in some way. I know that some were missed in this chapter and hope that they do not think me unkind or unappreciative. Thank you all.

On the production side of this book, thanks go to Darcy Marlow, assistant registrar at Philbrook Museum of Art in Tulsa, Oklahoma, for granting permission for the cover image *Slave Hunt, Dismal Swamp, Virginia*, painted by Thomas Moran in 1862. Jennifer Gallinger designed the cover and my appreciation is extended to her, to president Kirk Howard for believing in the merits of this project, to managing editor Shannon Whibbs for toiling on the final copy edits, as well as to all of the staff members at Dundurn who contributed in any way to this publication, particularly to two people who I have long admired and who championed this project — Barry Penhale, publisher emeritus, and wife, Jane Gibson, editor.

Final words of gratitude are reserved for a few special people: friends Lori Gardiner and Charles Brewer, wife Shannon and children Christopher, Justin, Melanie, and Rebecca for proofreading this manuscript, securing permissions for images, and for their unflagging support.

Bryan Prince

Notes

1. Letter to William Still from Francis Watkins Harper, describing her feelings upon first seeing Canada. This letter appeared in several publications, including Still's *The Underground Rail Road* (Philadephia: Porter & Coates, Philadelphia, 1872), 760.
2. Testimony of Susanna Brown, May 10, 1847. Pennsylvania State Archives. RG-26 Extradition files, Papers of the Governors. Courtesy of Karen James, also *Pennsylvania Freeman*, May 13, 1847.

Chapter 1: God Is Going to Trouble the Waters

1. Calvert County 1850. District 1 census, 19, lists 598 white males, 571 white females, 148 free "colored males"; 197 "colored females"; making a total of 1,514 free persons: 746 enslaved males, 768 enslaved females.
2. James Somervell, along with fifty-five other "Jacobite" prisoners, arrived in Maryland on October 18, 1716, aboard the ship *Good Speed*. Most were sold as indentured servants to serve a period of seven years. He later served as high sheriff of Calvert County. Immigrant Ships Transcribers Guild online courtesy of Michael A. Smolek (*www.immigrantships.net/v2/1700v2/goodspeed17161018.html#Somervell*).
3. 1840 U.S. Federal Census for Calvert County, 113; 1850 Calvert Personal Census, District 1, 13; 1850 Federal Slave Census for Calvert.
4. Copies of the 1780 Act for the Gradual Abolition of Slavery can be found online at: *www.ushistory.org/presidentshouse/history/gradual.htm* and the 1788 Amendment at *www.ushistory.org/presidentshouse/history/amendment1788.htm*.

5. Details of Charles S. Sewell's registration for four of his slaves can be found online at: *www.afrolumens.org/slavery/lancsy.html#Sewell,Charles S.*
6. Franklin Keagy, *A History of the Kagy Relationship in America from 1715 to 1900* (Albany: Joel Munsell's Sons, 1899), 437–38.
7. *Maryland Colonization Journal*, Vol. 2, No. 24 (June 1845): 384.
8. *Maryland Republican*, New Series, Vol. IV, Number 9 (November 1, 1845); *The New York Herald* (New York, Wednesday, October 29, 1845), Issue 278, Col D; *The Liberator* (Boston, Friday, November 7, 1845), Issue 45, Col D, 179; *The Boston Daily Atlas* (Thursday, October 30, 1845), Issue 104, Col C.
9. *Maryland Republican*, New Series, Vol. IV, No. 9 (November 1, 1845).

Chapter 2: And We Became Desperate

1. Mahommah Gardo Baquaqua and Samuel Moore, *Biography of Mahommah G. Baquaqua* (Detroit: Geo. E. Pomeroy & Co., 1854), 42–43.
2. Testimony of Lucinda Brown and Susannah Brown, May 10, 1847. Pennsylvania State Archives. RG-26 Extradition files, Papers of the Governors.
3. *Ibid.*
4. Governor Thomas G. Pratt, *Annual Message of the Executive to the General Assembly of Maryland. December Session, 1845* (Annapolis: Riley & Davis, Printers, 1845), 25–26.
5. *Baltimore Sun*, October 28, 1843, 2.
6. William I. Bowditch, *Slavery and the Constitution* (Boston: Robert F. Wallcut, 1849), 81.
7. Coverage of Isaac Brown's sworn affidavit appeared in several newspapers, including *Baltimore Sun*, May 25, 1847, and the *Philadelphia Ledger*, May 25, 1847. The United States Library of Congress has digitized a pamphlet on the Brown case that was originally printed by abolitionists in 1847 and has made it available on their American Memory website under the category of "Slaves and the Courts, 1740–1860." The title of the pamphlet is *Case of the Slave Isaac Brown: An Outrage Exposed* (*http://memory.loc.gov/ammem/sthtml/sthome.html*). Note that in Lucinda Brown's recollection of the events to the Pennsylvania court, she refers to the slave trader as "Hickman" Harris rather than "Samuel" Harris as his name appears in other records.
8. Joseph Sturge, *A Visit to the United States in 1841* (Boston: Dexter S. King, 1842), 30–33. See also *http://memory.loc.gov/cgi-bin/query/h?ammem/lhbtn-bib:@field(NUMBER+@band(lhbtn+00392))*.

9. *Frederick Douglass' Paper* (Rochester, NY), January 19, 1849, 1.

10. *Bangor Daily Whig & Courier* (Bangor, ME), August 22, 1855.

11. *The British Emancipator: Under the Sanction of the Central Negro Emancipation Committee* (London, UK) Issue XXXVI, Wednesday, January 23, 1839, 197. Reprinted from *Baltimore Democratic Herald.*

12. William Still's handwritten notes in Pennsylvania Abolition Society; "Journal C of Station No. 2 of the Underground Railroad (Philadelphia, Agent William Still) 1852–1857" In the Historical Society of Pennsylvania Collections (microfilm). See also the *Liberator*, (Boston), Issue 42, Col. A (Friday, October 20, 1843), 167. See also, John Wallace Hutchinson. *Story of the Hutchinsons (Tribe of Jesse).* 2 vols. Compiled and edited by Charles E. Mann, with an introduction by Frederick Douglass. (Boston: Lee and Shepard. 1896. Volume 1, Chapter 3, 100–01).

13. Daniel Drayton, *Personal Memoir of Daniel Drayton, for four years and four months a prisoner (for charity's sake) in Washington Jail* (Boston: Bella Marsh and New York: American and Foreign Anti-Slavery Society, 1855), 60. This document is online at the Library of Congress's American Memory website under "Slaves and the Courts. 1740–1860:" (*http://memory.loc.gov/ammem/sthtml/sthome.html*).The *Western Literary Messenger* (Buffalo, New York) also carried this passage on May 6, 1848.

14. Letter from an observer in Baltimore dated January 24, 1847, that originally appeared in London's *Anti-Slavery Reporter* and reprinted in *Emancipator and Republican*, April 21, 1847, 1.

15. Daniel Drayton, *Personal Memoir of Daniel Drayton*, 60.

16. New Orleans *Times-Picayune*, October 1, 1846.

17. New Orleans, *Courrier de la Louisiane*, April 15, 1845, and *Times-Picayune*, July 15, 1846.

18. Ralph Clayton, *Cash for Blood: The Baltimore to New Orleans Slave Trade* (Bowie, MD: Heritage Books, Inc., 2002). The original manifests for the *Victorine* and other ships from the port of Baltimore to New Orleans are in the U.S. National Archives and Records Administration, a part of Record Group 36, U.S. Customs Service Records, Port of New Orleans, Inward Slave Manifests. Clayton gives a glimpse of Slatter's slave pen and of his business dealings on pages 83–101 of this same book. Further information is in the classic work by Frederic Bancroft, *Slave Trading in the Old South* (1931; reprint, Columbia: University of South Carolina Press, 1996), 38, 121, 372–75.

19. L.A. Chamerovzow, ed., *Slave Life in Georgia: A Narrative of the Life, Sufferings, and Escape of John Brown, A Fugitive Slave Now in England* (London, UK: W.M. Watts, 1855) 112, 116.

20. National Archive Administration, Record Group 36; U.S. Customs Service Records Port of New Orleans, Louisiana; Inward Slave Manifests,1846; Roll #16.

21. *Baltimore Sun*, December 18, 1845, 1–2.

22. Pennsylvania State Archives, Testimony of Susanna Brown, May 10, 1847, RG-26 Extradition files, Papers of the Governors.

Chapter 3: Give Me Liberty

1. From William Wells Brown, comp. *The Anti-Slavery Harp* (Boston: Bela Marsh, 1848), 47.

2. *The Boston Daily Atlas*, , Issue 168, Col. H (Wednesday, January 14, 1846); New Orleans *Times-Picayune*, January 4, 1846.

3. Henry Benjamin Whipple, *Bishop Whipple's Southern Diary; 1843–1844* (1937; reprint edited by Lester B. Shippee) (New York: Da Capo Press, 1968), 118.

4. *Ibid.*, 112–13

5. William J. Anderson, *Life and Narrative of William J. Anderson, Twenty-four Years a Slave: Written by Himself* (Chicago: Daily Tribune Book and Job Printing Office, 1857), 22.

6. *Liberator*, (Boston) Issue 47, Col. C (Friday, November 19, 1841), 186, reported by Oliver Johnson. Shadrack was advertising his own business in Macon, Georgia, as early as May 5, 1832, when he ran advertisements in the *Macon Weekly Telegraph*, noting that he specialized in "young negroes." Both he and Hope Slatter were partners by the next year, *Macon Weekly Telegraph*, November 14, 1833.

7. L.A. Chamerovzow, ed., *Slave Life in Georgia: A Narrative of the Life, Sufferings, and Escape of John Brown, A Fugitive Slave Now in England* (London, UK: W.M. Watts, 1855), 115–17.

8. Among the 1846 issues of the *Courier* that carried the advertisement were January 3, 7, and 24, February 24, and May 14, 15, 18, and 26.

9. A detailed map that pinpoints the location of William Kenner's farm is held by the Library of Congress and is online at: *http://usgwarchives.org/ maps/louisiana/statemap/1858brno.jpg* and identified as *LA-MS 1858 —* 1,136k. Baton Rouge to New Orleans showing land owners. Modified from *Norman's Chart of the Lower Mississippi River* by A. Persac. Engraved, printed, and mounted by J.H. Colton & Co., New York. The 1840 slave census lists Kenner as having ninety-seven slaves; the 1850 census lists 114 slaves.

10. Jim Davis, *History of Kenner: The Early Years* (see *www.eastjeffersonparish. com/history/KENNER/EARLY/EARLY.HTM*).

11. Craig A. Bauer, "From Burnt Canes to Budding City: A History of Kenner Louisiana," *Louisiana History: The Journal of the Louisiana Historical Association*, Vol. 23, No. 4 (Autumn 1982): 358.

12. Stanley Clisby Arthur and George Campbell Huchet de Kernion, *Old Families of Louisiana* (Gretna, LA: Pelican Publishing Company, 1998), 157–60.

13. New York's *Emancipator* newspaper of February 1, 1844, reported one such case where Slatter conditionally sold a "bright mulatto girl" from Louisiana to Dr. Buckner of Mississippi who was visiting Baltimore, for $500 on a trial basis. Should the girl be deemed suitable, the sale would be completed upon the doctor's return to Mississippi.

14. U.S. Army Corps of Engineers, New Orleans District, *Cultural Resource Survey and Testing of the East Jefferson Parish Levee Gap Closure*, Final Report, April 1992 (*www.dtic.mil/cgi-bin/GetTRDoc?AD=ADA250137& Location=U2&doc=GetTRDoc.pdf*).

15. Craig A. Bauer, "From Burnt Canes to Budding City, A History of Kenner Louisiana," *Louisiana History: The Journal of the Louisiana Historical Association*, Vol. 23, No. 4 (Autumn, 1982): 360.

16. Paul Tenkotte, professor of history at Thomas More College, provided details in his article "A Legend in Ludlow," published in *Cincinnati Magazine*, Vol. 36, No. 4 (January 2003): 93–96.

17. Junius P. Rodriguez includes this case, known as "The German Coast Insurrection" in *Encyclopedia of Slave Resistance and Rebellion*, Vol. 2 (Westport, CT: Greenwood Press, 2007), 616. Slaves Guiau and Harry, who belonged to William Kenner Sr. and his partner Stephen Henderson, were sentenced to death. Bausson, a third slave of theirs, was returned to jail because the charges against him seemed "vague and of little certainty."

18. Frederick Douglass, *My Bondage and My Freedom* (New York and Auburn: Miller, Orton & Mulligan, 1855), 301.

19. Interview with Thomas Smallwood, American Freedmen's Inquiry Commission, 1863, part of *War Department, Letters Received by the Adjutant General*, National Archives, Washington, D.C.

Chapter 4: By the Law of Almighty God

1. Benjamin Drew, *The Refugee: or the Narratives of Fugitive Slaves in Canada* (1856; reprint, Toronto: Dundurn Press, 2004).

Notes

2. E.L. Carey and A. Hart, *Philadelphia in 1830–1 or a brief account of The Various Institutions and Public Objects in this Metropolis* (Philadelphia: n.p., 1830), 70–71.

3. Compiled under the direction of the Society of Friends, *A Statistical Inquiry into the Condition of People of Colour of the City and Districts of Philadelphia* (Philadelphia: Kite & Walton, 1849), 29–44.

4. This advertisements appeared for weeks in the *Pennsylvania Freeman*, including on February 26, 1846.

5. *Niles National Register* (Report of the Postmaster General), December 20, 1845, 254. The closest post office to Alexander Somerville's was at St. Leonard.

6. *Session Laws of Maryland, 1841–42*, Chapter 272, Section 3, as quoted by Clement Eaton in *The American Historical Review*, Vol. 48, No. 2 (January 1943): 269.

7. These details surface in an interview with Thomas Smallwood, "American Freedmen's Inquiry Commission, 1863," part of "War Department, Letters Received by the Adjutant General," National Archives, Washington, D.C.

8. Of the many newspapers across the country that covered the case, the *National Anti-Slavery Standard*, New York, September 30, 1847, appears to be among the most reliable for intimate details.

9. Coverage of Governor Pratt's runaway or "kidnapped" slave Sophia story appeared in the *Baltimore Sun*, April 24, 28, and May 1, 1846.

10. Maryland State Archives, Proceedings of the Governor 1839–1861, M3162: (*www.msa.md.gov/megafile/msa/speccol/sc4800/sc4872/html/executive.html*, 433).

11. *Evening Bulletin* (Philadelphia), May 3, 1847; *The North American* (Philadelphia), May 4, 1847, Issue 2519, Col. C; *Spirit of the Times and Daily Keystone* (Philadelphia), May 4, 1847; and the *Baltimore Sun*, May 4 and 5, 1847. Location of northeast station on Cherry Street, west of Fourth, determined in the *Journal of the Common Council of the City of Philadelphia 1847–1848* (Philadelphia: King and Baird, 1848), 200.

12. June 24, 1847, minutes from Abolition Society meeting. Microfilm copy at Purdy-Kresge Library at Wayne State University, Detroit. Original in Historical Society of Pennsylvania, Philadelphia.

13. *The Pennsylvanian*, May 5, 1847, and *Pennsylvania Freeman*, May 6, 1847.

14. Robert Davison Coxe, *Legal Philadelphia: Comments and Memories* (Philadelphia: William J. Campbell, 1908), 153.

15. *Ibid., passim*; R.C. Smedley, *History of the Underground Railroad in Chester and the Neighboring Counties of Pennsylvania* (1838; reprint, Mechanicsburg, PA: Stackpole Books, 2005), 235, 345. John Smith Futhey and Gilbert Cope, *History of Chester County, Pennsylvania*; Vol. 2

(Philadelphia: Louis H. Everts, 1881), 568–69.

16. *Public Ledger* (Philadelphia), Mary 5, 1847; *Pennsylvania Freeman*, *Baltimore Sun*, and *Albany Evening Journal* (reprinting article from *Philadelphia Bulletin*), May 6, 1847; *National Era* (Washington, D.C.), May 13, 1847.

17. Following the passage of the Fugitive Slave Law in 1850, Edward Duffield Ingraham was appointed United States commissioner to rule on fugitive slave cases. One of his more memorable rulings was the sending of a suspected runaway back to his master in Maryland, only to have the master declare that it was the wrong man and was not his slave.

18. Ingraham married Caroline Barney from Baltimore on September 15, 1836.

19. Charles Gibbons's handwritten notes on the testimony held in the Pennsylvania State Archives, and *Evening Bulletin*, May 6, 1847.

20. *Baltimore Sun*, May 7, 1847.

21. Pennsylvania State Archives, Charles Gibbons to Francis R. Shunk, May 5, 1847, RG-26 Extradition files, Papers of the Governors.

22. *Ibid.*, Thomas Earle to Francis Shunk, May 5 and 10, 1847.

23. Signatures courtesy of Pennsylvania State Archives and Karen James, Pennsylvania State Archives, RG-26 Extradition files, Papers of the Governors.

24. *Ibid.*, James Mott to Francis Shunk, May 5, 1847.

25. *The Pennsylvanian*, May 14, 1847, carried Champneys's opinion, dated May 4, and Shunk's letter to Pratt dated May 5. The runaways were John Mack, Samuel Lockman, Ellen Lockman, and her sons Henry and James.

26. *Public Ledger and Daily Transcript* and *The Pennsylvanian* May 8, 1847; *Baltimore Sun* May 12, 1847; *Pennsylvania Freeman*, May 20, 1847; and *Case of the Slave Isaac Brown: An Outrage Exposed*, an eight-page pamphlet published by members of the Pennsylvania Anti-Slavery Society that detailed the case. This is available online through the Library of Congress's American Memory website at: *http://memory.loc.gov/cgi-bin/query/r?ammem/llstbib:@field(TITLE+@od1(Case+of+the+slave+Isaac+Brown+:+))*.

27. *Spirit of the Times*, May 5, 1847.

28. *Philadelphia Freeman*, August 12, 1847. The Anti-Slavery Society for Eastern Pennsylvania, New Jersey, and Delaware, whose members included some of the Philadelphia supporters of Isaac Brown, was involved in distributing petitions and advocating changes to Pennsylvania laws concerning slavery and fugitives.

29. Philadelphia Society for Alleviating the Miseries of Public Prisons, *Journal of Prison Discipline and Philanthropy*, Vol. 1, (1845): 244–45. Details of the prison population and recent deaths were provided by Kristy Johnston in "The Case of Isaac Brown" prepared for Villanova University as part of a larger work: *In Pursuit of Liberty: African American Court and Prison*

Stories from Philadelphia 1820's to 1840's. Ms Johnston cites "Prison Society Records May 1847" housed at Pennsylvania Historical Society. Description of the cells appears in Daniel Bowen, *A History of Philadelphia: With a Notice of Villages in the Vicinity* (Philadelphia: n.p., 1839), 180–82.

30. *Chatham Gleaner* (Ontario), November 2, 1847, quoting from an unnamed Syracuse newspaper.
31. *Public Ledger*, May 7 and 10, 1847. *North American*, May 11, 13, 17 and 22, 1847. There is a particularly interesting account in the May 18th entry in the diary of Thomas P. Coke, which is online at the tri-college (Haverford, Swarthmore, and Bryn Mawr) digital library: *http://triptych.brynmawr.edu/index.php.*
32. *Pennsylvania Freeman*, May 13, 1847.
33. *Baltimore Sun*, May 15, 1847, and the *Niles National Register* (Baltimore), May 22, 1847.
34. Pennsylvania State Archives, *State of Maryland vs. Isaac Brown*, May 10, 1847, RG-26 Extradition files, Papers of the Governors.
35. *Public Ledger*, May, 25, 1857.
36. Pennsylvania State Archives, Requisition from Governor Shunk to Judge Parsons, May 19, 1847, RG-26 Extradition files, Papers of the Governors.
37. J.J. Robbins, *The Pennsylvania Law Journal*, Vol. VI (Philadelphia: I.Ashmead, Printer, 1847), 414–15. New Series Vol. I.

Chapter 5: Let My People Go

1. *Baltimore Sun*, May 25, 1847, *Star & Banner* (Gettysburg) and *Star*, May 28, 1847. The sheriff of Philadelphia was Henry Lelar, Esquire.
2. *Spirit of the Times* (Philadelphia), May 24, 1847.
3. *Ibid.*, May 25, 1847.
4. *National Anti-Slavery Standard*, September 30, 1847.
5. *Public Ledger*, May 25, 1847, and *Pennsylvania Freeman*, May 27, 1847. The letter was written by J. Simon Cohen, the prothonotary (chief clerk) of the Supreme Court of Pennsylvania, Eastern District.
6. Philadelphia *Sun*, May 23, 1847.
7. Copies of Brown's affidavit appeared in several newspapers including *Pennsylvania Freeman*, May 27, 1847.
8. *Pennsylvania Freeman*, May 27, 1847. *Public Ledger*, May 25, 1847, as noted in the pamphlet, *Case of the Slave Isaac Brown: An Outrage Exposed*.
9. Philadelphia *Sun*, May 25, 1847, and *Pennsylvania Freeman*, May 27, 1847.

10. *Daily Picayune*, June 3, 1847.
11. *Pennsylvania Freeman*, May 27, 1847.
12. June 24, 1847, minutes from Abolition Society meeting. Microfilm copy at Purdy-Kresge Library at Wayne State University, Detroit. Original in Historical Society of Pennsylvania, Philadelphia.
13. Isaac T. Hopper to Sarah H. Palmer, June 15, 1847, online at the tri-college (Haverford, Swarthmore, and Bryn Mawr) digital library, see *http://triptych. brynmawr.edu/index.php;* and Lucretia Mott to Nathaniel Barney, June 7, 1847, see *http://www.mott.pomona.edu/lettertonbarney.htm.*
14. *Pennsylvania Freeman*, July 8, 1847. Little Wesley may well have been the church that the Brown family would have attended when they lived in Philadelphia.
15. *Ibid.*
16. *Pennsylvania Freeman*, July 8 and 15, 1847; *The New York Herald*, July 14, 1847; *Non-Slaveholder*, August 1, 1847; and both *Liberator* and *Daily Picayune*, July 23, 1847.

Chapter Six: One More River to Cross

1. Thomas Wentworth Higginson, *Army Life in a Black Regiment* (Boston: Lee & Shephard; New York: Charles T. Dillingham, 1890), 204.
2. *Liberator* (Boston), Friday, May 21, 1847, Issue 21, 82; and *Liberator*, Friday, June 4, 1847, Issue 23, 92; Note that at this convention new officers were elected — Frederick Douglass was elected president, Francis Jackson, James Mott, and Edmund Quincy became vice-presidents and Lucretia Mott was elected to the business committee
3. *Ibid.* Note that the other fugitive was Lewis Hayden.
4. *Pennsylvania Freeman*, September 30, 1847.
5. Hiram Wilson to George Whipple, August 6, 1847, American Missionary Association Papers (Canada).
6. *Liberator*, October 15, 1847.
7. Hiram Wilson's trip to Boston is mentioned in *Liberator*, April 23, 1847, and *Emancipator*, June 9, 1847. Henson's visit appears in *Emancipator*, May 12, 1847, and *National Era*, June 3, 1847. Henson, who had arrived in Boston prior to May 3, was still there on May 26, so it is possible that he may have met Isaac Brown.
8. Josiah Quincy had also displayed his support for the anti-slavery cause a year earlier by giving free railroad passage to Hiram Wilson, along with

three hundred pounds of baggage filled with donations to Canadian fugitives, *Liberator*, June 12, 1846. Quincy was also one of the driving forces behind building the Western Railroad Corporation, which later became the Boston and Albany Railroad.

9. For a good description of the entire route, see William Guild, *A Chart and Description of the Boston and Worcester and Western Railroads* (Boston: Bradbury & Guild, 1847). Available on Google Books.

10. *Albany Evening Journal*, July 23, 1847.

11. *National Anti-Slavery Standard*, September 30, 1847. Please note that this newspaper is the source of all upcoming details of the Brown's flight from Boston to Canada.

12. *New York Herald*, July 11, 1847.

13. *National Era*, May 18, 1848, May 20, 1847, and *Emancipator and Republican*, May 21, 1845.

14. Luther Lee, *Autobiography of Luther Lee* (New York: Phillips & Hunt, 1882), 332.

15. *New York Spectator*, June 13, 1839.

16. *Albany Evening Journal*, October 10, 1835.

17. *Ibid.*

18. *Albany Evening Journal*, May 18, 1850. Confirmation of Wilkinson's change of views appear in Jermain Loguen's autobiography, *The Rev. J. W. Loguen As A Slave And A Freeman* (Syracuse, NY: J.G.K. Truair & Co., 1859), 364.

19. *Frederick Douglass' Paper*, October 8 and 15, 1852.

20. *National Anti-Slavery Standard* (New York), September 30, 1847.

21. *Ibid.* The kindly stranger's name was Henry Bush.

22. *Emancipator* and *Milwaukee Sentinel*, July 21, 1847; *National Era*, July 22, 1847; *New Hampshire Sentinel*, July 29, reprinted the article from Alabama.

23. *National Anti-Slavery Standard*, September 30, 1847.

24. John L. Myers, "American Antislavery Society Agents and the Free Negro 1833–1838," *Journal of Negro History*, Vol. 52, No. 3 (July 1967): 215–18.

25. Hannah Wilson's obituary was printed in *Christian Guardian*, August 25, 1847.

26. *Emancipator*, June 9, 1847, and *Liberator*, June 5 and 25, 1847.

27. *Signal of Liberty* (Ann Arbor, MI), February 16 and October 31, 1846.

28. Roman J. Zorn, "An Arkansas Fugitive Slave Incident and its International Repercussions," *The Arkansas Historical Quarterly*, Vol. 16 (Summer 1957): 139–49. For Stewart's report on the case, see *Emancipator*, September 15, 1842.

29. *The Anti-Slavery Reporter*, July 1, 1851, carried the story (reported by Hiram Wilson) of a runaway slave who was held on the same Arkansas plantation as Nelson Hackett.

30. David G. Chardavoyne, *A Hanging in Detroit: Stephen Gifford Simmons and the Last Execution under Michigan Law* (Detroit: Wayne State University Press, 2003), 120.
31. *National Anti-Slavery Standard*, September 30, 1847. Identity of Lewis (Louis) Davenport confirmed in *Signal of Liberty* (Ann Arbor, MI), March 9, 1842.

Chapter 7: The Sun Came Like Gold Through the Trees

1. Sarah H. Bradford, *Harriet: The Moses of Her People* (New York: Geo. R. Lockwood & Sons, 1886), 30.
2. Anna Jameson, *Winter Studies and Summer Rambles in Canada*, Volume 2 (New York: Wiley and Putnam, 1839), 85.
3. *National Anti-Slavery Standard*, September 30, 1847.
4. American Missionary Association Archives (Canada), Hiram Wilson to George Whipple, August 6, 1847.
5. *Signal of Liberty*, November 3, 1845, and *National Era*, November 18, 1847. The rope makers are identified as George Cary and Charles Harrison in the *Chatham Gleaner*, August 17, 1847.
6. *National Era*, April 8, 1847.
7. *Sun*, December 4, 1847.
8. *Pennsylvania Freeman*, September 9, 1847.
9. This segment of the letter appeared in *Liberator*, October 15, 1847.
10. Elma E. Gray, *Wilderness Christians: The Moravian Mission to the Delaware Indians* (1856; reprint, New York: Russell & Russell, a division of Antheneum Press, 1973), 292.
11. *National Anti-Slavery Standard*, September 30, 1847.

Chapter 8: Rescue the Slave

1. *Provincial Freeman*, September 8, 1855.
2. The *Globe*, December 11, 1847, carried a rebuke of Henry Sherwood and praise for William Badgley. This was written by a delegation of forty-six people from Toronto, including local black leader, Wilson Ruffin Abbott. The men who gave letters of support for Young's character included Hiram Wilson; Colonel John Prince, representative for Essex County in the provincial legislature; Charles H. Stewart, Esquire, from Detroit,

and several other American abolitionists, including Isaac Hopper.

3. *New York Daily Tribune*, October 1, 1847, (reprint of article that was credited as having originally appeared in the Canadian newspaper, the *Galt Reporter*, *Boston Daily Courier*, September 27, 1847; *Trenton State Gazette*, September 27, 1847; *Pennsylvania Freeman*, September 30, 1847, and October 7, 1847; *Emancipator* (New York), October 6, 1847; *Toronto Banner*, September 17, 1847; *Boston Daily Transcript*, October 5, 1847, *Liberator* (Boston), October 1 and 15, 1847; *North Star* (Rochester, New York), September 7, 1849.

4. *Liberator* (Boston), October 15, 1847.

5. *Globe*, December 11, 1847, and The Hiram Wilson Papers, Oberlin College, Ohio.

6. For a thorough and wonderfully written book on this area, see Linda Brown-Kubisch, *The Queen's Bush Settlement: Black Pioneers 1839–1865* (Toronto: Natural Heritage Books, 2004).

7. *True Wesleyan*, August 28, 1847.

8. Fidelia Coburn Brooks to Lewis Tappan, October 14, 1847. Coburn and Brooks were married on October 6, 1847; American Missionary Association papers (Canada).

9. *Liberator*, October 15, 1847.

10. The death of Samuel Young was widely reported in newspapers on both sides of the border. In addition to those newspapers mentioned previously, the *Toronto Mirror* of October 15, 1847, reprinted the notice that had appeared in the *Galt Reporter*. *National Anti-Slavery Standard* (New York), September 30, 1847, and *Liberator* of October 15, 1847, published the most comprehensive and reliable accounts based on details that had been provided by Samuel Young and Hiram Wilson. It was determined that he had contracted typhus or "ship-fever" days earlier from the dying Irish immigrants in Montreal.

Chapter 9: But the Conflict Will Be Terrible

1. John Quincy Adams, "Diary in Abridgment," December 1, 1821– December 31, 1838 (with gaps), 687 (electronic edition, *www.masshist.org/ jqadiaries*). *The Diaries of John Quincy Adams: A Digital Collection* (Boston: Massachusetts Historical Society, 2004).

2. *Pennsylvania Freeman*, August 12, 1847.

3. *Toronto Banner*, September 17, 1847.

4. *Pennsylvania Freeman*, September 30, 1847.

5. *New York Tribune*, October 1, 1847, carried the previously published *Toronto Banner* article.
6. *Toronto Mirror*, October 15, 1847, carried the previously published *Galt Reporter*. The *Liberator*, October 29, 1847, carried the *Christian World* article. The *National Anti-Slavery Standard*, September 30, 1847, appealed to its readers to contribute either through their office or to William E. Whiting from the American Missionary Association.
7. *Liberator*, September 24 and October 15, 1847.
8. Annual Message to the General Assembly, Public Documents 1847 A, Maryland State Hall of Records, Accession No. MdHR 812036, Location 2/1/7/26, PD570.
9. *Ibid.*
10. *Pennsylvania Freeman*, January 6, 1848.
11. J. Thomas Scarf, *History of Maryland from the Earliest Period to the Present Day*, Volume 3 (Baltimore: John. B. Piet, 1879), 331–32.
12. Lucretia Mott to Joseph and Ruth Dugdale, March 28, 1849. Published in *Selected Letters of Lucretia Coffin Mott*, by Beverly Wilson Palmer ed., (Champaign: IL: University of Illinois Press, 2003), 180. In addition to the case of Isaac Brown, Mott also singled out the stories of Henry "Box" Brown who had escaped by getting into a box and having himself shipped from Virginia to Philadelphia, and William and Ellen Craft who openly fled from slavery by having the fair-skinned Ellen dress as a man and pretend that William was her servant and travelling companion.

Chapter 10: Many Thousand Gone

1. Wilson's character and motives were often attacked in the press: *The Oberlin Evangelist*, December 20, 1843, Volume V, No. 26, 20; American Missionary Association letter from Isaac Rice to Brother Harned, November 24, 1847.
2. James C. Brown relates this and other observations on the Dawn Settlement in the *Chatham Tri-Weekly Planet*, January 10, 1860.
3. Lewis Tappan to Hiram Wilson, April 25, 1848, Library of Congress, The Tappan Papers, *Letterbook*, November 4, 1847–June 30, 1852.
4. Hiram Wilson to George Whipple, February 29, 1848, AMA Papers (Canada).
5. Hiram Wilson to George Whipple, May 1, 1848, AMA Papers (Canada).
6. Hiram Wilson to George Whipple, December 21, 1848, January 8 and 16, 1849, and July 4, 1850.

7. The chapter on Queen's Bush that appears in Benjamin Drew's 1856 publication, *The Refugee: or the Narratives of Fugitive Slaves in Canada*, contains several first-hand accounts of the changing conditions experienced by those who lived there. On pages 120–24 of her 2004 groundbreaking work, *The Queen's Bush Settlement: Black Pioneers 1839–1865*, Linda Brown-Kubisch wrote of the decline of the population and of John and Fidelia Brooks's move to Africa. In addition to Brown-Kubisch's work, the American Missionary Association papers contain copious details of the problems at Queen's Bush immediately following Isaac Brown's arrival in Canada, that is, the letter from Isaac Rice to Brother (illegible) November 24, 1847.
8. *The Voice of the Fugitive*, April 22, 1852.
9. *The Voice of the Fugitive*, April 23, 1851, gives the black population of Chatham as "near seven hundred individuals."
10. *Frederick Douglass' Paper*, August 24, 1855.
11. Article written by abolitionist Reverend Samuel J. May for the *National Anti-Slavery Standard* and reprinted in *Frederick Douglass' Paper*, August 27, 1852.

Chapter 11: Something to Hope For

1. Samuel Gridley Howe, *Report to the Freedmen's Inquiry Commission, 1864, The Refugees from Slavery in Canada West* (1864; reprint, New York: Arno Press and the *New York Times*, 1969), 28.
2. Archives of Ontario, Marriage Records of Western District 1786–1856, Microfilm MS 205, Reel #13. Note that this entry is among those on images # 157–59 submitted by Reverend Fear under the heading "returns only not in register."
3. Full text of quote from Samuel Ringgold Ward, regarding Edwin Larwill, from *Autobiography of a Fugitive Negro: His Anti-Slavery Labours in the United States, Canada, & England*, (1855), 28:

> I must be allowed to express my regret that some of the black men of Chatham — men, too, of wealth and position, as compared with many others, white and black — are wanting in manliness. They do not bravely, manfully, stand up for themselves and their people as they should. They cower before the brawling demagogue Larwill — a man well known as an enemy of the Negro, but a man beneath any manly Negro's contempt — a recreant Englishman, of low origin but aspiring tendencies,

not knowing his place, and consequently not keeping it. He has some little property, some coarse vulgar talent, which, with a good degree of dogged boldness, makes him—especially as his principles are of most convenient changeableness — popular with his class. It was he who moved, as an appendix to the vote ratifying Lord Elgin's Reciprocity Treaty, a provision against fugitives entering Canada except under onerous Negro-catching conditions. He avowed his object to be, to please the slaveholders of America. English readers will pardon me for obtruding so unworthy a man upon their notice; but I am sure they will at the same time approve my scolding black men for cringing to him, much more for voting for him, when a candidate for office. I say, this man and all like him should be taught that the self-respect of every black man, imperatively forbids his having anything to do with them; much less seeking their favour, by anything like fawning upon them.

4. Public Archives of Canada, William King Collection, R4402-0-1-E. Petition to the Presbyterian Synod. Available on Microfilm Reel C-2223 and online at: *www.lac-bac.gc.ca/northern-star/033005-119.01-e.php?&fond_id_nbr=1&m_t_nbr=3&fond_seq=1_3_15&sk=11&s=3c&&PHPSESSID=u90qkpunk9kus3e7528q7godp6.*

5. This information appears in the research notes of John Brown scholar and collector Boyd B. Stutler, whose collection is held by West Virginia Division of Culture and History. Much of this amazing collection has been digitized and is online at: *www.wvculture.org/history/wvmemory/imlsintro.html.* The specific note describing the Charity Building is at *www.wvculture.org/history/wvmemory/jbdetail.aspx?Type=Text&Id=2443.*

6. These instructions appear in Samuel Thomson's thirteenth edition of *The Thomsonian Materia Medica*, published in 1841. For a comprehensive look at the Thomsonian methods, see the link posted by the South West School of Botanical Medicine on the Life and Times of Samuel Thomson: *www.swsbm.com/ManualsOther/Samuel_Thomson-Lloyd.pdf.*

Chapter 12: I Can Do My Own Thinkings

1. Benjamin Drew, *The Refugee: Or the Narratives of Fugitive Slaves in Canada* (Boston: John P. Jewett and Company, 1856), 177.

2. *Provincial Freeman*, July 26, 1856.

3. Letter from Chatham teacher James Grant to Henry Bibb for publication in *Voice of the Fugitive*. In 1851, there were two schools for blacks in Chatham. *Voice of the Fugitive*, April 9, 1851, 3.

4. Donald Simpson, *Under the North Star: Black Communities in Upper Canada* (Trenton, NJ: Africa World Press, 2005), 318.

5. *Provincial Freeman*, May 30, 1857, 1, and *Voice of the Fugitive*, April 23, 1851.

6. *Provincial Freeman*, June 20, 1857, 2.

7. *Liberator*, October 7, 1859, January 13, 1860, and February 28, 1862.

8. *Liberator*, April 11, 1862.

9. *Provincial Freeman*, March 14, 1857, 2.

10. Benjamin Drew, *The Refugee: Or the Narratives of Fugitive Slaves in Canada* (Boston: John P. Jewett & Co., 1856), 234. Drew published sixteen of the interviews that he conducted in Chatham — unfortunately neither Samuel nor Susannah Russell was included. In his preface, Drew stated that he had many more that could not fit into one volume, but hoped to publish them in the future. He never did, and, tragically, to date, his papers remain lost.

11. Drew, *The Refugee*, 236.

12. *Chatham Weekly Planet*, August 9, 1860.

13. James A. Handy, *Scraps of African Methodist Episcopal History* (Philadelphia: A.M.E. Book Concern, 1902), 213–16. Digitized at "Documenting the American South" (*http://docsouth.unc.edu/church/handy/handy.html*).

14. Donald Simpson, *Under the North Star: Black Communities in Upper Canada* (Trenton, NJ: Africa World Press, 2005), 329.

15. This September 1858 case was extensively covered by newspapers in Canada and the United States, but with contradictory information. For an analysis of the case, see The Black Abolitionist Papers: Canada, 392–98.

16. *Recollections of Edwin Bassett Jones*, 24–26. In 1924, one hundred copies were printed by his daughter Grace Jones Morgan.

17. *Provincial Freeman*, June 7, 1856, 2.

Chapter 13: The River Jordan Is Muddy and Cold

1. Currency charts and average Canadian pay appeared in the *Provincial Freeman* on August 22, 1855.

2. A brief biography of John Drake appears on page 448 of *The John Askin Papers*, Volume 1, edited by Milo M. Quaife, Detroit Library Commission,

1928. A sketch of John Drake and his son Francis appears on page 351 of *The Valley of the Lower Thames: 1640 to 1850* by Fred Coyne Hamil, published by the University of Toronto Press in 1951. Reprinted in 1973.

3. One example is the farm of Abraham Shadd (the father of Mary Ann and Isaac) who lived four miles south of the land attributed to Samuel Russell. Shadd's one hundred acres was assessed at 180 pounds. Fifty-acre farms within the Buxton Settlement were often assessed at sixty pounds.

4. This tax book is in the archives at Buxton National Historic Site & Museum, North Buxton, Ontario.

5. *Provincial Freeman*, April 25, 1857.

6. An Ontario Ministry of Natural Resources report, written in 1998 by Patrick McLean and entitled "The Evolution of a Prairie Landscape Over Time in Raleigh Township, Kent County," describes the changes in the Raleigh Plains over time. This report appears online at: *http://nhic.mnr.gov.on.ca/MNR/nhic/documents/spring1999/spring99.htm* Descriptions of children being lost appear in several sources including page 60 of *Historical Atlas of Essex & Kent Counties 1880–1881*, published by H. Belden & Co. of Toronto.

7. Patrick Ryan to Commissioners of Crown Lands, February 13, 1855. The reply from the attorney general is undated. Both documents appear in "The Township Papers: Raleigh" microfilmed copy in the Kent Genealogy Society collection at the Chatham Public Library.

8. Sheriff Mercer to Duncan McGregor, deed registered at the Kent County Registry Office in Chatham in Book O, Folio 159, #158.

9. Kent Registry Office, John Fleming to Samuel Russell, Document 193, Volume C, Folio 214.

10. Kent Registry Office, Samuel Russell to Henry Ruttle, Document 194, Volume C, Folio 216.

Chapter 14: Somber Skies and Howling Tempests

1. *Frederick Douglass' Paper*, November 9, 1855.

2. Signed on behalf of the First Coloured Baptist Congregation in Chatham by M.F. Bailey, C.H. Charity, M.A. Johnson, James Snyder, Bazzell Bell, J.C. Brown, *Provincial Freeman*, August 8, 1857, 1. Cornelius H. Charity was the brother of James Charity, who owned the building where the Shadds had their offices. Cornelius purchased James's business when his brother left Chatham.

3. *Provincial Freeman*, May 19, 1855.

4. The section on Chatham is part of a much larger article that William Wells Brown wrote for the *Pine and Palm*, the official journal of James Redpath's Haytian Emigration Bureau, organized to promote North American black immigration to Hayti. The entire article is reprinted in *The Black Abolitionist Papers, Volume 2, Canada, 1830–1865*, C. Peter Ripley, ed. (Chapel Hill and London: University of North Carolina Press, 1986), 471–73. The University of Toledo has digitized an interesting online exhibit written by Barbara Floyd on the history of medicine entitled "From Quackery to Bacteriology: The Emergence of Modern Medicine in 19th Century America: An Exhibition" (*www.utoledo.edu/library/canaday/exhibits/quackery/quack1.html*).

    From a twenty-first-century perspective, it is interesting to note that Wells Brown had high praise for Dr. Alexander T. Augusta, who graduated with a Bachelor of Medicine degree from Trinity College at the University of Toronto, whom he described as "a physician of decided merit" despite that doctor advertising the old-fashioned methods of "cupping, bleeding" and "leeches applied."

5. Thomas Hersey, senior ed., *The Thomsonian Recorder*, Vol. 2, No. 12, (March 15, 1834), 188; and Vol. 2, No. 19 (June 21, 1834), 289–94 (*http://books. google.ca/books?id=_cYWAAAAYAAJ&pg=PR12&lpg=PR12&dq=%22S amuel+Thomson%22+%22scarlet+fever%22&source=bl&ots=BmJTKuUW Wg&sig=vLwCldwQckgZdXlRxT1h7TDAr64&hl=en&ei=B_w1Td2_ BITGlQeWrKiBCg&sa=X&oi=book_result&ct=result&resnum=1&ved=0CB oQ6AEwAA#v=onepage&q=%20%22scarlet%20fever%22&f=false*).

6. *New Albany Daily Ledger*, May 29, 1860.

7. 1861 Census of Canada, Ontario, District 1, Harwich Township, page 12. (Note that Jacob is also enumerated in his father's household in Chatham District 2, page 43.)

Epilogue: The Last Mile of the Way

1. 1871 Census of Canada, Ontario, Kent District 2, Chatham sub-district G, 155.

2. The unnamed child's birth and death are registered under Ontario Births #038093.

3. The death of this unnamed infant is recorded as March 20, 1873, Ontario Schedule of Deaths, Kent, Town of Chatham, 204.

4. Annie Maria Russell died August 4, 1875. Ontario Schedule of Deaths for 1875, Kent, 46.

5. 1881 Census of Canada, Ontario, Chatham, District 180, 45. 1891 Census, Kent District 79, Chatham sub-district B, 31.
6. Ontario Schedule of Deaths for 1883, Kent, 276.
7. 1880 Kent Directory, (for Town of Chatham) Jacob Russell, col'd, labourer, lives 416 Wellington St. E. 1885–86 *The Chatham Directory and County Gazeteer,* Jacob Russell, labourer, lives 39 Prince St. *Union Publishing Co's Chatham Directory For 1895-6;* Jacob Russell, whitewasher, h. 273 King St. E. 1891 Census, Canada, Ontario, Chatham Town, Film # T-6345, Division 2, 31.
8. Ontario Death Schedule for 1896, Kent, Town of Chatham, 424 (apoplexy was the name given for a stroke).
9. 1870 census for Wayne County Michigan, Detroit Ward 7, 212. Elizabeth's maiden name determined by 1904 marriage registration of their thirty-seven-year-old daughter, Eliza J. to Thomas H. Williams, both of Detroit, in Essex County. Undated on *www.ancestry.com*, but appears in Essex Schedule B, 458.
10. *Charles F. Clark & Co.'s Annual City Directory 1871–72,* 374. *J. W. Weeks & Co's Annual City Directory of Detroit for 1873–74,* 474. *Hubbell & Weeks Annual City Directory of the City of Detroit, 1872–73,* 429.
11. U.S. Federal Mortality Schedules, 1880, Michigan, Wayne County, Detroit Enumeration District 275, 1.
12. 1880 census for Wayne County, Michigan Detroit, District 275, 38. (Note the daughter's names — Catharine, seventeen; Elisa, fifteen; and Idell, thirteen — have a different spelling than the 1870 census.)
13. *Detroit Free Press,* January 5, 1887, 4, under title LOCAL BREVITIES.
14. Ontario Marriages 1801–1926, #003435, Essex County. The marriage took place on December 12, 1887.
15. 1861 Census of Canada, Kent County, Harwich Townships, 12 and 13.
16. Bureau of Refugees, Freedmen and Abandoned Lands, 1865–1869, NARA Microfilm publication M1055, Roll 21 (*http://freedmensbureau.com/washingtondc/outrages2.htm*). The assault on Isaac Brown was made by Calvin Robinson on August 9, 1865.
17. Bureau of Refugees, Freedmen and Abandoned Lands, 1865–1869, NARA Microfilm publication M1055, Roll 21 (*http://freedmensbureau.com/washingtondc/outrages2.htm* and *http://freedmensbureau.com/washingtondc/outrages.htm*).
18. 1860 Personal and Slave Census and 1870 Personal Census for Calvert County.
19. Information provided through a brief history of Middleham Chapel Episcopal Church available at the church.

20. Slatter's retirement was published in several newspapers including Boston's *Evening Transcript*, June 23, 1848, and the *Liberator*, May 25, 1849. According to published reports in the July 14, 1848, and January 19, 1849, issue of *Frederick Douglass' Paper*, Slatter made a final lucrative and well-publicized transaction in April of 1848 when he marched fifty-two slaves — captured after their failed mass escape attempt aboard the schooner *Pearl* — through Washington, D.C., en route to Baltimore where they were shipped to New Orleans.

21. *Baltimore in 1846* by Henry Stockbridge as it appeared in *Maryland Historical Magazine*, Vol. IV, 27.

22. This article, originally written to the editor of the *Commonwealth*, was widely reprinted as front page news including in the *Wesleyan*, October 20, 1853, and the *Liberator*, October 7, 1853. A contradictory article appeared earlier in the July 23, 1847, edition of the *Liberator*, which stated that President Polk did indeed ride in Slatter's carriage.

23. Article from the New Orleans *Picayune* that was reprinted in the *Philadelphia Inquirer*, September 21, 1853, 1. The purchase of this edifice known as "the Banking House of the Branch of the State of Alabama" was reported in the *Alexandria Gazette*, September 9, 1850, and the *Daily Alabama Journal*, September 23, 1850. According to Washington's *Daily National Intelligencer*, March 21, 1860, as well as the *Picayune*, he also owned a theatre in Mobile.

24. Note that in the 1871 census for Harwich Township, Sarah is listed as thirty-six years old, and in 1881 census she is forty-six.

25. Isaac and Susannah Brown's names recorded in the Archives of Ontario, Toronto, Marriage Registrations: Office of the Registrar General; (RG 80-5); Microfilm group MS932, Reel 5, 352.

Selected Bibliography

Anderson, William J. *Life and Narrative of William J. Anderson, Twenty-four Years a Slave: Written by Himself.* Chicago: Daily Tribune Book and Job Printing Office, 1857.

Bacon, Margaret Hope. *Valiant Friend: The Life of Lucretia Mott.* New York: Walker and Company, 1980.

Bancroft, Frederic. *Slave Trading in the Old South.* Columbia, SC: University of South Carolina Press, 1996. Reprint.

Bauer, Craig A. "From Burnt Canes to Budding City: A History of Kenner Louisiana." *Louisiana History: The Journal of the Louisiana Historical Association,* Vol. 23, No. 4 (Autumn 1982): 353–81.

Bibb, Henry. *A Narrative of the Life and Adventures of Henry Bibb.* New York: n.p., 1849.

Buck, Rev. D.D. *Progression of the Race in the United States and Canada.* Chicago: Atwell Printing and Binding Co., 1907.

Buckingham, James Silk. *The Slave States of America.* Bedford, MA: Applewood Books, 1842.

Carey, E.L., and A. Hart. *Philadelphia in 1830–1, or a Brief Account of the Various Institutions and Public Objects in This Metropolis: Forming a Complete Guide for Strangers, and a Useful Compendium for the Inhabitants.* Philadelphia: n.p., 1830.

Chamerovzow, L.A., ed. *Slave Life in Georgia: A Narrative of the Life, Sufferings, and Escape of John Brown, A Fugitive Slave Now in England.* London, 1855.

Chardavoyne, David G. *A Hanging in Detroit: Stephen Gifford Simmons and the Last Execution under Michigan Law.* Detroit, MI: Wayne State University Press, 2003.

Clayton, Ralph. *Cash for Blood: The Baltimore to New Orleans Slave Trade.* Bowie, MD: Heritage Books, Inc., 2002.

Clisby, Stanley Arthur, and George Campbell Huchet de Kernion. *Old Families of Louisiana.* Gretna, LA: Pelican Publishing Company, 1998.

Selected Bibliography

Coxe, Robert Davison. *Legal Philadelphia: Comments and Memories.* Philadelphia: William J. Campbell, 1908.

Douglas, R. Alan, ed. *John Prince: 1796–1870.* Toronto: University of Toronto Press, 1980.

Douglass, Frederick. *My Bondage and My Freedom.* New York and Auburn, NY: Miller, Orton & Mulligan, 1855.

Drayton, Daniel. *Personal memoir of Daniel Drayton, for four years and four months a prisoner (for charity's sake) in Washington jail.* Boston: B. Marsh and New York for American and Foreign Anti-Slavery Society, 1855.

Drew, Benjamin. *The Refugee: or the Narratives of Fugitive Slaves in Canada.* Boston: John P. Jewett & Co., 1856.

Eaton, Clement. "Censorship of the Southern Mails." *The American Historical Review,* Vol. 48, No. 2 (January 1943): 266–80.

Gray, Elma E. *Wilderness Christians: The Moravian Mission to the Delaware Indians.* Ithaca, NY: Cornell University, 1856.

Guild, William. *A Chart and Description of the Boston and Worcester and Western Railroads.* Boston: Bradbury & Guild, 1847.

Hallowell, Anna Davis (editor of her grandparent's writings). *James and Lucretia Mott: Life and Letters.* Boston: Houghton, Mifflin and Company, 1884.

Hamil, Fred Coyne. *The Valley of the Lower Thames: 1640 to 1850.* Toronto and Buffalo: University of Toronto Press, 1951.

Handy, James A. *Scraps of African Methodist Episcopal History.* Philadelphia: A.M.E. Book Concern, 1902.

Haviland, Laura. *A Woman's Life-Work.* Cincinnati: Walden and Stowe, 1882.

Jameson, Anna. *Winter Studies and Summer Rambles in Canada.* Vol. 2. New York: Wiley and Putnam, 1839.

Johnson, Walter. *Soul by Soul: Life Inside The Ante-bellum Slave Market.* Cambridge, MA: Harvard University Press, 2001.

Jourdan, Elise Greenup. *Settlers of Colonial Calvert County, Maryland.* Lewes, DE: Colonial Roots, 2001.

Kubisch, Linda Brown. *The Queen's Bush Settlement: Black Pioneers 1839–1865.* Toronto: Natural Heritage Books, 2004.

Lauriston, Victor. *Romantic Kent: The Story of a County, 1626–1952.* 1952. Reprint, Chatham, ON: Chamberlain/Mercury Printing, 1996.

Lee, Luther. *Autobiography of Luther Lee.* New York: Phillips & Hunt, 1882.

Loguen, Jermain. *The Rev. J.W. Loguen as a Slave and a Freeman.* Syracuse, NY: J.G.K. Truair & Co., 1859.

Nash, Gary B. *Forging Freedom: The Formation of Philadelphia's Black Community.* Cambridge, MA: Harvard University Press, 1988.

Needles, Edward. *The Pennsylvania Society for Promoting the Abolition Of Slavery.* New York: Arno Press, 1969.

Newman, Richard S. *Freedom's Prophet: Bishop Richard Allen, the AME Church, and the Black Founding Fathers.* New York: New York University Press, 2008.

Palmer, Beverly Wilson, ed. *Selected letters of Lucretia Coffin Mott.* Champaign, IL: University of Illinois Press, 2002.

Pease, William and Jane. *Black Utopia.* Madison, WI: The State Historical Society of Wisconsin, 1963.

Quaife, Milo M., ed. *The John Askin Papers.* Volume 1. Detroit: Detroit Library Commission, 1928.

Ripley, C. Peter, Roy Finkenbine et al. *The Black Abolitionist Papers: Volume II.* Chapel Hill and London: North Carolina Press, 1886.

Rhodes, Jane. *Mary Ann Shadd Cary: The Black Press and Protest in the Nineteenth Century.* Bloomington and Indianapolis, IN: Indiana University Press, 1998.

Scarf, J. Thomas. *History of Maryland from the Earliest Period to the Present Day.* Volume 3. Baltimore: John. B. Piet, 1879.

Shippee, Lester B., ed. *Bishop Whipple's Southern Diary: 1843–1844.* 1937. Reprint, New York: Da Capo Press, 1968.

Siebert, Wilbur H. *The Underground Railroad from Slavery to Freedom.* New York: The Macmillan Company, 1898.

Simmons, William J. *Men of Mark: Eminent, Progressive and Rising.* Cleveland: Geo. M. Rewell & Co., 1887.

Simpson, Donald. *Under the North Star: Black Communities in Upper Canada.* Trenton, NJ: Africa World Press, 2005.

Society of Friends. *A Statistical Inquiry into the Condition of People of Colour of the City and Districts of Philadelphia.* Philadelphia: Kite & Walton, 1849.

Sterling, Dorothy. *The Making of an Afro-American: Martin Robison Delany, 1812–1885.* Garden City, NY: Doubleday, 1971.

Ullman, Victor. *Look to The North Star: A Life of William King.* Boston: Beacon Press, 1969.

Ward, Samuel Ringgold. *Autobiography of a Fugitive Negro: His Anti-Slavery Labours in the United States, Canada, & England.* London: John Snow, 1885.

Zorn, Roman J. "An Arkansas Fugitive Slave Incident and its International Repercussions." *The Arkansas Historical Quarterly*, Vol. 16, No. 2 (Summer 1957): 139–49.

Index

Index

Index

Index

About the Author

Author photo courtesy of Casey Narcis and Eva Niederdorfer of Studio Nostalgia, Toronto, Ontario, www.studionostalgia.ca.

Bryan Prince is a much-respected historical researcher with a particular interest in the Underground Railroad, slavery, and abolition. The author of two bestselling books, *I Came as a Stranger* and *A Shadow on the Household*, he is much in demand as a presenter throughout Canada and the United States. Prince and his wife, Shannon, were awarded the 2011 prize for the "Advancement of Knowledge" by the *Underground Railroad Free Press*. They live in North Buxton, Ontario.

Of Related Interest

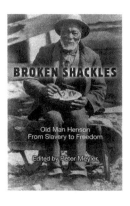

Broken Shackles
Old Man Henson from Slavery to Freedom
by John Frost, edited by Peter Meyer
978-1896219578
$22.95

In 1889, *Broken Shackles* was published in Toronto under the pseudonym of Glenelg. This very unique book, containing the recollections of a resident of Owen Sound, Ontario, an African American known as Old Man Henson, was one of the very few books that documented the journey to Canada from the perspective of a person of African descent. Henson was a great storyteller and the spark of life shines through as he describes the horrors of slavery and his goal of escaping its tenacious hold.

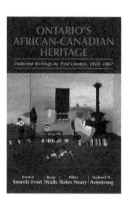

Ontario's African-Canadian Heritage
Collected Writings by Fred Landon, 1918-1967
Edited by Karolyn Smardz Frost, Bryan Walls, Hilary Bates Neary,
and Frederick H. Armstrong
978-1550028140
$28.99

Ontario's African-Canadian Heritage is composed of the collected works
of Professor Fred Landon, who for more than sixty years wrote about
African-Canadian history. The selected articles have, for the most part,
never been surpassed by more recent research and offer a wealth of data
on slavery, abolition, the Underground Railroad, and more, providing
unique insights into the abundance of African-Canadian heritage in
Ontario. This volume, illustrated and extensively annotated, includes
research by the editors into the life of Fred Landon.

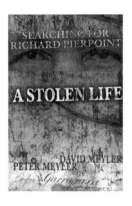

A Stolen Life
Searching for Richard Pierpoint
by David Meyler and Peter Meyler
978-1896219554
$19.95

Richard Pierpoint or Captain Dick, as he was commonly known, emerges from the shadows of history in *A Stolen Life: Searching for Richard Pierpoint*. An African warrior who was captured at about age sixteen, Pierpoint lived his remaining years in exile. From his birth in Bundu (now part of Senegal) around 1744, until his death in rural Ontario in 1837, Pierpoint's life allows us to glimpse the activity of an African involved in some of the world's great events.

Available at your favourite bookseller.

What did you think of this book?
Visit www.dundurn.com for reviews, videos, updates, and more!